FAVORITE
DOG HIKES
IN AND AROUND
LAS VEGAS

FAVORITE
DOG HIKES
IN AND AROUND
LAS VEGAS

WYNNE BENTI
MEGAN LAWLOR

SPOTTED
DOG PRESS.
BISHOP

Favorite Dog Hikes In and Around Las Vegas

©2005 Wynne Benti

Published exclusively by Spotted Dog Press, Inc., Bishop, California
Spotted Dog Press is a registered trademark of Spotted Dog Press, Inc.

ISBN 1-893343-10-3
1st edition 2006
Please write us at:
Spotted Dog Press
P.O. Box 1721
Bishop CA 93515
800-417-2790
FAX 760-872-1319
store@spotteddogpress.com
Book design and layout by Spotted Dog Press, Inc.

Library of Congress Cataloging-in-Publication Data
Benti, Wynne.
    Favorite dog hikes in and around Las Vegas / Wynne Benti, Megan Lawlor.
      p. cm
    Includes bibliographical references (p.) and index.
    ISBN 1-893343-10-3
    1. Hiking with dogs--Nevada--Las Vegas Region--Guidebooks. 2. Trails--Nevada--
    Las Vegas Region--Guidebooks. 3. Las Vegas Region (Nev.)--Guidebooks. I. Lawlor,
    Megan 1959- II. Title

    SF427.455.B46 2005
    796.5109793135--dc22

                                    2005044627

Printed in the United States of America

A Note About Safety

Hiking can be a risky sport associated with many hazards including, but not limited to, those mentioned in this book: heat and heat-related injuries (heat exhaustion, heat stroke), dehydration, adverse weather conditions, snake bites, insect bites, animal bites, slipping, falling or other types of injury, potential contact with unsavory characters and canines. The hikes in this book have been rated for difficulty. Please note the difficulty rating of each hike and do not hike above your or your dog's skill level. There is no substitute for experience, skill, knowledge of safety procedures and common sense! The publisher and authors of this guide make no representation as to the safety of any hiking or driving route described herein. Conditions are constantly changing. Before you hike, we recommend consulting current maps, local road and weather conditions, and contacting the supervising land agency for updates on any trail, road, fire or other closures.

A Word About Archaeological Sites and Artifacts

*Archaeological sites and artifacts are protected
by the Antiquities Act of 1906
and the Archaeological Resources Protection Act of 1979.
All historic and prehistoric sites on federal lands
are protected and defacement, removal,
excavation or destruction of such antiquities is prohibited by law.*

Jim, Rosy and Doug en route to Mummy Spring via Trail Canyon PHOTO: Wynne Benti

TABLE OF CONTENTS

"MY BURRO AND I, AND A LITTLE DOG,
ARE GOING ON AND ON, UNTIL SOONER OR LATER,
WE REACH THE END OF THE HORIZON."

EVERETT RUESS, 1931
TRAVELING IN THE SOUTHWEST
WITH HIS DOG, CARLY

THE HEROIC DOG

FOREWORD

Las Vegas has long been famous for its spectacular resorts and night-life. The gaming, the shows and an endless array of great restaurants have made Las Vegas a top destination spot for people all over the world. As the population here grows by hundreds of thousands, it doesn't take much imagination to understand that without water and electricity from the Colorado River, the city would cease to exist as we know it. There is no doubt, however, that the natural inherent beauty that surrounds Las Vegas and on which the city is built would endure.

Just beyond Las Vegas lies a land of immense beauty and uniqueness. Ancient peoples, explorers, miners and settlers have lived or traveled through this valley leaving traces of their past. The sandstone temples of Red Rock Canyon, the forested snow-capped peaks of the Spring Mountains, the desert lakes and hidden oases, all are a day's journey or less waiting to be explored.

The stark desert may seem void of life to the first-time visitor. If you venture into the Sheep Mountains for example you may wonder why they call it a wildlife refuge. You might ask, "Where is the wildlife?"

It's not only at the hotels, *it is out there.*

Coyote, fox, mountain lion, tortoise, big horn sheep, lizards and snakes, all sorts of exotic little creatures, and hundreds of species of birds—exist within the vast terrain of diverse and complex life. Though they may elude your gaze on the first scan, you will discover their unique needs. The big horn require tremendous spaces just to wander, to exist, without human interference, and for no other reason than their survival.

To the northwest, you and your dog will discover the amazing Spring Mountains. A lush green "island" bursting forth from the desert floor, these mountains support an enormous wealth of life. A wonderful place to hike, they offer picturesque, challenging peaks and refreshing, often hidden streams. Connecting these mountains, to the south, is the stunningly beautiful Red Rock Canyon. It's magnificent geology, almost a half billion years old in some places, has created a natural treasure trove of scenic colorful trails beckoning you and your

dog to enjoy and explore.

For me, after a week of work, nothing is quite so wonderful as the solitude and quiet of the desert lowlands where one's gaze can stretch for miles as one inhales the soothing scents of desert sage. While growing up in Las Vegas can have its highs and lows, I've never grown tired of exploring its great, grand outdoors.

Years of great weekend adventures have led to many wonderful memories shared with family and life-long friends, and those memories are still being created. My family's dogs have been a BIG part of these ventures and have inspired us to get out and hike. Dogs are great at getting you off the couch. I've never met a dog that didn't enjoy going for a walk. They also keep you from getting fat by sharing your sandwich.

Most of our dogs came from shelters. My last dog Ginger, bless her sweet soul, was already five years old when I adopted her. The wonderful thing about adopting an older dog is that they usually don't have to be housetrained. And I really do believe they know you are saving their life. She was a very gentle and loving dog and super with my little daughter.

In this book, you'll find our favorite dog-tested places. We've noted where water is available, what is the best season to hike, and what is the relative "toughness" of the terrain. Those questions are answered in the satisfaction we see and feel in our own lives and in the behavior of our best friends.

So, put on your hiking boots, pack your leash and water bowl and come, enjoy the magnificent outdoors, the Las Vegas that truly stays here, eternally. — *Megan Lawlor*

O who will walk a mile with me
Along life's merry way?
A comrade blithe and full of glee,
Who dares to laugh out loud and free,
And let his frolic fancy play,
Like a happy child, through the flowers gay
That fill the field and fringe the way
Where he walks a mile with me.

And who will walk a mile with me
Along life's weary way?
A friend whose heart has eyes to see
The stars shine out o'er the darkening lea,
And the quiet rest at the end o' the day,--
A friend who knows, and dares to say,
The brave, sweet words that cheer the way
Where he walks a mile with me.

With such a comrade, such a friend,
I fain would walk till journeys end,
Through summer sunshine, winter rain,
And then?—Farewell, we shall meet again!

A Mile With Me by Henry Van Dyke

INTRODUCTION

Most of the hikes for this book were scouted in summer, beginning at dawn or a few hours before sunset. It rained the first two weeks of August. Each day clouds of rain moved across the great sandstone cliffs of Red Rock, cooling canyon walls and rocks. Our dogs played in the big watery puddles that formed on the uneven trail as we listened to rainmade waterfalls cascade and echo off the high sandstone cliffs inside Pine Creek Canyon.

Daily afternoon thunderstorms in the Spring Mountains were predictable but never expected. In a cold wet hailstorm we watched lightning strike on either side of the summit register box on Charleston Peak. We weren't deterred from making the dash, dogs and all, to sign the register, to leave a washer and a rock as a symbol—*we were here.*

One night, I met up with a friend at Bonnie Springs, a classic Las Vegas watering hole and sat down on the barstool next to him. Immediately, he and the bartender pointed out that the seat I was sitting in was reserved, that I couldn't sit there. Then I noticed the "reserved" placard solemnly placed between the salt and pepper shakers and bottles of ketchup. A half hour later, a tiny elderly woman came in and climbed up on the barstool. Hanging on the wall behind her were pictures of a beautiful young woman dancing, ice-skating, performing—full of life. It was her, Bonnie Levinson, the petite woman now sitting next to me on the reserved barstool. Born in a hospital off Hollywood Boulevard in Los Angeles, her father worked for the studios. It was only natural that the business of entertainment would be her destiny. In 1950, she arrived in Las Vegas. A young woman, just turned thirty, she bought the 115 acres on which the Bonnie Springs hotel was built for $24,000. There was plenty of water but no power. She bought a liquor license and opened her back-country desert bar. Howard Hughes was her neighbor.

It wasn't that long ago that the only way to get to Red Rock was by dirt road. Town ended at Upland and from there it was wide open desert as far a you could see. Now it is covered by tract neighborhoods and multi-million dollar homes. There were no gates, no fences and no *no trespassing signs*. Then, the desert belonged to everyone.

While scouting the North Peak trail off the Rocky Gap 4x4 Road, I high-centered my Jeep on the Pahrump side of Red Rock Summit where heavy winter storms washed out the road. Despite the road conditions on the Pahrump side of the Rocky Gap 4x4 road (maybe one day there will be money in the BLM and USFS budgets to repair the historic road again), we included North Peak in this guide with plenty of warnings about the road. It's just such a lovely hike. I learned that when you drive backcountry roads be prepared to get yourself out. If I carried a larger jack I probably would have been able to get the Jeep over the hump. Instead I hiked back to North Peak, called the Auto Club on my cell phone, naively thinking they were experienced in such matters and could drop off a jack or bring a truck in with a winch. When the driver couldn't find me, the Auto Club called the Las Vegas Metro Police Department's Search and Rescue unit. If I had only followed the advice I give in this book—don't travel alone and carry a big Hi-Lift jack!

At age eleven, I "won" my first dog, a sweet little mutt I named Mitzi, by paying twenty-five cents for a surprise envelope on a tree at a street fair in New York City. My first officially adopted dog came from the Yolo County animal shelter near Sacramento, years later while I was going to school at the University of California, Davis. Since then, I brought five more into my family. Each dog has hiked the trails with me and each has made a notable canine mountain ascent, including White Mountain Peak (14,256') just south of Boundary Peak, Nevada's highest. All were the inspiration for my first dog hiking book, *Favorite Dog Hikes In and Around Los Angeles* written in 1995, the first regional dog hiking guide of its kind in the country. ***Favorite Dog Hikes In and Around Las Vegas*** was next, a project I had dreamed of writing for years. But the entire process was beset by delays, the kind that interrupt most of life's best laid plans.

By the time the book was finished, cancer claimed my husband's life; my Jeep got wedged into a couple of tight mountain squeezes requiring extraction; one of the computers we used to produce the book gave up its silicone ghost; another got a nasty virus that began to erase a year's worth of writing and a third computer was shorted out by an electrical storm.

Between Megan and I, three of our old dogs passed away—good lives well lived—but necessitated the immediate adoption of a new

canine hiking generation. The topper came when two writers contacted Spotted Dog Press about writing a generic Las Vegas hiking guide. As my husband lay dying and with no hope of finishing *Favorite Dog Hikes In and Around Las Vegas* anytime soon, I suggested they write my dog hiking guide since the best generic Las Vegas hiking guides were already written by Branch Whitney. Instead, they took the whole thing to another publisher, hiking shoes, barking dogs and all. In short, it seemed like it took a lifetime of dog days to get this book to press—but we did it, thanks to my coauthor, Megan Lawlor, born and bred in the heart of Las Vegas.

In the end, **Favorite Dog Hikes In and Around Las Vegas** was about the most fun I've ever had writing a book (with the exception of **Favorite Dog Hikes In and Around Los Angeles**). I met many great people on the trail and would like to thank the Lawlors, the Vegas Valley 4-Wheelers, Edwin Moradian and Las Vegas Metro Police Department SAR and the very dog-friendly Bonnie Springs.

Without the dogs there would have been little inspiration to write this guide. It is our hope that everyone who uses this book has as much fun as we did walking the trails on our **Favorite Dog Hikes In and Around Las Vegas!** — *Wynne Benti, Publisher*

BACKCOUNTRY
BASICS
FOR YOU AND YOUR DOG

Sharing the Trail with Others

We started hiking these trails in the 1970s, when it was a real desert wilderness experience. In fact, the road into Red Rock was gravel, and most of the canyon trails were just two track Jeep trails. Las Vegas was the Strip and Red Rock was much further away from town, making it even more remote than it is today. It seemed to take forever to get up Mt. Charleston Blvd. The trails were empty save for the rare sighting of someone else out in their CJ5 exploring the desert. It was rare to run into anyone. Not anymore!

Back then, perhaps a few investors ever foresaw the housing boom that has occurred over the past ten years. Those that did thought it would happen much sooner. There was a lot more open space and desert to cross—now it's all houses!

During the past decade, all of the trails in this book have grown hugely in popularity as have the ways in which people use them. We share the trails with other dogs and people of all ages and interests, mountain bikers, climbers, hikers, people who like dogs and don't like dogs, burros and native wildlife including rattlesnakes, coyotes and mountain lions.

The most important verbal command to teach your dog for wilderness travel is "come!" When you shout your dog's name along with that word, your dog should forego all other distractions and return to you at once. A dog's ability to respond to that one simple command could mean the difference between life or death.

For most of us, leashes are the best way to keep our dogs close. Hands-free leashing, which requires snapping a rock climbing carabiner to your belt loop or pack belt and clipping your dog's leash into the carabiner, is a great way to keep your dog close and your hands free for cross-country scrambling and maneuvering.

Dogs have individual personalities. Their unique responses to situations along the trail may at times be difficult to predict, particularly if they are unleashed. Many times, a dog's worst enemy on the trail, with the exception of rattlesnakes and ticks are unleashed dogs not under their master's verbal control.

A word here about mountain bikers. Mountain bikers really can come down a trail so quickly and quietly, that they are never seen or heard until they are right on top of you and your dog, making it easy for a person or dog to inadvertently wander into the path of a mountain bike. Be aware of this especially on popular trails. The more you are aware of what's going on around you, the safer and happier you and your dog will be.

OTHER DOGS

Plenty of other folks with their dogs will be hiking the trails, sharing your love of wild places. You'll be surprised at the vast array of canine types, an assortment of sizes, shapes and personalities, some friendly, some not so friendly, and the unsocialized or aggressive dog not conditioned as a pup to being around people or other dogs. Dogs that have not been socialized should always be leashed.

There is the story of Bart, the Rottweiler. The ancient Roman Army

PHOTO: Megan Lawlor

used Rottweilers to guard their cattle and protect their camps. Bart loved to hike, but spent most of his life in the backyard. Never socialized with other dogs or people for that matter, he wanted to dominate everything. He wasn't trained to be aggressive— he had never been socialized. Knowing his disposition, his owners always kept him leashed in public. This didn't keep other unleashed dogs from coming over to him, but they didn't hang around long.

Dogs test other dogs to determine their place in the pack. On leash or off, unless dogs are trained to stay, dogs will run over to other dogs. It's just instinct. It's a rare dog that's oblivious to the presence of other dogs. We can't stress how important it is to socialize dogs with people and other dogs. Our Las Vegas dog parks are an excellent place to do this.

Oh Behave! Socialize Your Dog!

Socialize your dog at an early age. Get them out and around other dogs, people and children. Dog parks and obedience classes are excellent venues for socializing dogs, the earlier in a dog's life, the better. Obedience classes take an average of six weeks. Dogs and owners are all together learning the basics of good behavior: how to sit, stay, come, and walk on leash. Socializing will help your dog feel comfortable around other canines and with a little obedience training thrown in, will minimize future aggressive behavior.

Only you know your dog. With the knowledge you have of your pet, you should always be prepared to deal with any unexpected situation encountered on or off the trail.

Hands-Free Leashing

A sturdy leash is essential for any dog hike. Visit the rock climbing section of your local outdoor store and buy a carabiner, unlocking or locking. KMART stocks small brightly colored carabiners at the

checkout stands. Attach the carabiner to a belt loop on your shorts or around the fastened belt of your day pack or fanny pack. Put the end of your dog's nylon leash inside the carabiner and snap it shut.

When I wear a day pack, I attach carabiners to my pack's waist belt, then attach one, two or more dogs to my waist on each carabiner. They pull me up the mountain trails and they love it! It's a team, it's dog our pack. I know exactly where they are all the time and can easily reel them in when needed.

When traveling in Las Vegas desert country be aware of snakes, burros, and coyotes. Dogs will pounce on a rattlesnake before you can say "no!" A rattlesnake bite will kill a dog. Burros will chase and kick a dog thinking it a predator.

Hands-free leashing

We have known people whose dogs have been killed or injured by the swift kick of a burro or range cow.

Dog owners have a great responsibility on and off the trail to always keep their four-legged hiking companions close to them and under control.

PET ID TAG

Our vet surgically implanted a recovery microchip in the back of Rosy's neck which will identify her if taken to a vet's office or shelter with a scanner. There are two tags on her collar—a county dog license and an engraved identification tag with my name and phone number.

WATER! WATER! WATER! (AND A SPORTS DRINK!)

Water, a lightweight plastic or nylon collapsible bowl and a sturdy leash are essential on any hike. In a pinch, a plastic lunch bag can double as a make-shift bowl. We cannot stress the importance of having enough water for you and your dog to prevent heat illness (heat exhaustion and stroke) and dehydration!

Natural water sources in the desert are slim to none. Red Rock National Conservation Area recommends drinking four liters (the size of two large soda bottles) per day, the same or more for your dog. As you get to hiking with your dog on known trails, you'll get a better idea of how much water you'll both need, by knowing how long the hike will take and what the prevailing weather conditions will be.

In Grand Canyon National Park, the National Park rangers stress the importance of adding an electrolyte replacement powder to your water or replace one liter of water with a liter of sports drink. At the Grand Canyon, they have a problem with hyponatremia, a physical condition that occurs when people drink so much water, without any electrolyte additive, they actually become dehydrated and fatigued.

Needed electrolytes and minerals are being flushed out by water and not being replenished. We always mix a small amount of Gatorade in our dog's water for that extra energy boost.

Water weighs about 1.75 pounds per quart, and depending on where you hike, you'll be carrying a day's worth of water for both of you. In late spring through early fall plan walks early in the morning (with a pre-dawn start if possible) and in the early evening, after the sun has dropped below the mountains.

Before the gates open at dawn, there is often a line of cars waiting along SR-159 to get into Red Rock. Get an early start for longer hikes and go on cool days. Summer hiking with a dog in Las Vegas is impossible unless you head high in the Spring Mountains, or get super early morning starts or hike before dusk. Summer hiking in Red Rock is pleasant with an early start (off trail by 9 a.m.) and at dusk. Your dogs will let you know whether or not they want to join you—they won't want to leave the comfort of the air-conditioned house on hot days. On the way to the car, ours will stop, sit down and won't move an inch.

Recommended Water Quantities

If you want your pet to carry it's own water, purchase a dog pack, one with good padding on the chest and back straps. Before you leave home, familiarize your dog with its new pack. Put the pack on your dog to get the right fit, then try it with a load. Take your dog for a walk to work out any tailoring problems before hitting the trail.

Recommended minimum quantities for canine water are listed under each hike in this book. These recommended amounts are based on the needs of a medium-sized dog weighing about thirty-five pounds in moderate temperatures (65-70 degrees). Every dog has different needs and it will be up to you to determine how much water your dog will need.

Carry at least an extra gallon of water in your car either in an ice chest or wrapped up in a heavy blanket or sleeping bag for insulation on warm Las Vegas days. Large, collapsible plastic water containers (from 2.5 gallons and up) are available at outdoor equipment stores. Dogs welcome a cold drink of water back at the car after a long, hard dusty hike.

The Mouse's tank—a murky desert waterpocket at trail's end   PHOTO: Wynne Benti

DESERT WATER SOURCES

Never depend on natural water sources for your water supply, even if one is noted on your topo map. Actually, we might extend that to any water source, including fountains at dog runs, many of which were dry when we scouted them for this book.

Streams may be dry any time of the year or unfit for consumption. People should never drink from any natural, unfiltered water source in any wilderness location in the west. Sadly, most streams contain bacteria and other stuff that can cause various intestinal ailments with such unpleasant symptoms as abdominal pain, gas, diarrhea, or worse. Some friends still drink out of the streams in the Spring Mountains. They say, that compared with the water in Lake Mead that eventually becomes city drinking water, the water in local mountain streams is really not the bad.

One particularly nasty bug, *Giardia lamblia*, found in human and animal waste, is a main source of contamination these days. The microscopic *Giardia* cysts can be effectively removed from potential drinking water with a portable water filter, purchased at an outdoor store. Water filters are typically used on extended backpacking trips when it's not convenient to carry the additional weight of bottled water or when not enough water can be carried for the duration of the trip.

Giardiasis is something you don't want to get as it has many disagreeable symptoms like acute abdominal pain, severe intestinal gas and bloating, as well as recurrent diarrhea and vomiting, that can last up to three to four weeks. The worst case scenario is a stay in the hospital. According to our vet, dogs can get *Giardiasis* and other ailments from drinking contaminated water. If a dog becomes infected, symptoms will include diarrhea and vomiting. Contact your vet immediately to obtain treatment.

One of the other notices you'll see posted at various thermal water sources is a warning about *Naeglieria fowleri*. Naeglieria is a common genus of soil and freshwater amoebo-flagellate with only a few of the species actually pathogenic in humans and animals. *N fowleri* is one of these. This amoeba can live many generations without ever infecting a host. In humans, the amoeba are thought to enter the brain through the nose while swimming in warm water. They destroy red blood cells and brain tissue causing Primary Amoebic Meningoencephalitis (PAM). To date there have been 300 human cases recorded worldwide with only seven folks surviving the PAM infection. The first recorded case in the United States occurred in 1966. According to Asad Khan MD, Department of Internal Medicine, Division of Infectious Diseases, Louisiana State University Health Science Center:

"Most *N fowleri* infections have occurred in children and young

Warning at Rogers Spring in Lake Mead NRA
PHOTO: Wynne Benti

adults who have had recent exposure to swimming or diving in warm fresh water. The thermophilic nature of *N fowleri* allows it to survive in waterways contaminated by thermal discharges from power plants, heated swimming pools, and even hot springs with temperatures up to 45°C (113°F). Most cases of PAM occur during the summer months when freshwater sources are warm. When water temperatures decrease, *N fowleri* encyst and enter a dormant stage, which allows them to survive until the next summer."

Though clinical infection with *N fowleri* is exceptionally rare (as noted above with 300 documented cases worldwide), it has one of the highest mortality rates of any infectious disease. Survival depends on early and correct diagnosis and immediate treatment.

Get into Condition and Keep Fit!

Everyone (dogs and people) should be in good physical condition before embarking on most of the hikes in this book. A dog can be just

PHOTO: Wynne Benti

as out-of-shape as a person and in need of physical conditioning. Both need to build strength and endurance for hiking. It is incredibly difficult to carry an exhausted thirty-five pound dog five miles back to the car, let alone a heavier one.

Start your conditioning regimen by trying a few of the easy hikes listed in this book, then move on to the more difficult ones. There are easy hikes in both Red Rock and the Spring Mountains. Any trip can be a challenge if you or your dog are not in shape.

The key to training is to start off flat and easy, eventually adding mileage and hills to build endurance and to do it regularly. Below is a basic regimen that will help you and your dog get started:

Suggested Training Regimen

First week: Easy walks 3 times a week minimum. Around the block is fine.

Second week: Continue the easy walks. Add one long walk with ups and downs increasing mileage to 1-2 miles or increase the number of short walks.

Third week: Continue daily walks. Add one moderate hike with hills, about 400-800 feet of gain with more mileage, and carry 2 liters of water in a daypack on your back. Carrying a daypack is a great way to build strength. Do this once a week plus the flat walks.

Fourth week: Note your progress. Are you and your dog ready for more difficult hikes? Monitor your progress and keep on walking!

There are plenty of hikes for your old dog as Duke will attest PHOTO: Megan Lawlor

What About My Old Dog?

During my seminars on dog hiking someone will always ask, "What about my old dog?" An old hiking dog may never lose the desire to want to go with you and there are plenty of hikes in this book perfect for an old dog and for you! Though he may not be able to keep up on the difficult trails any longer, there are many easy walks for just your older dog. The Ash Grove Nature Trail in Spring Mountain Ranch is a lovely walk as is Wheeler Camp, and all of the hikes in Cold Creek.

Older dogs don't have to walk very far to be happy. The most important thing is to just get them out. I'll take my oldest dog to Wheeler Camp. We walk a short distance to shade and water. I carry a collapsible lawn chair and set up my chair. I sit while she sniffs at her own pace, then usually lays down, and is just happy to be out.

First Aid

Many items in a first aid kit for people work on a dog. A roll of one inch waterproof tape, some 2.25" x 3" medium adhesive pads and one or two rolls of gauze come in handy for taping sensitive paw pads or barbed wire accidents. An anti-bacterial ointment like neosporine can be used to disinfect scrapes and cuts. Tweezers can be used to remove ticks or cactus spines; needle nose pliers for removing stubborn cholla and cactus spines if hiking in the desert. If your dog wears hiking boots to protect his paws, carry a spare set just in case one is lost or torn.

Evacuating Your Dog

A word here about evacuating your dog. Dogs can tire much more quickly on long hikes than their owners and may need a lift from time to time. Trying to carry them out may be difficult. One friend carried her dog on her shoulders, wrapped around her neck like a scarf. Others have loaded small dogs in their packs.

If your dog gets sore paws, is injured, or becomes too tired to walk back to the car, be prepared to handle the situation. If you and your dog are in good physical condition, the chances of this happening will be greatly reduced.

LVMPD Search & Rescue coming into Red Rock Visitor Center PHOTO: Wynne Benti

BACKCOUNTRY RESCUES

The trips in this book require a lot of backcountry travel and the chances are that if you become stranded most likely it's going to happen in your car. Before traveling any desert road make sure to carry a few basic items in your vehicle:

- water (we carry 2.5 gallons minimum)
- anti-freeze
- quart of engine oil
- small shovel and two 2x4 boards, 3-4 feet in length
- good size tire jack–we recommend a Hi-Lift jack as most standard jacks that come with vehicles are inadequate in high-center situations.

Land management agencies around Las Vegas do not handle any search and rescue operations. All rescue operations are coordinated by the Las Vegas Metropolitan Police Department's Search and Rescue unit and initiated with a call to 911. The general rule of thumb if your vehicle gets stuck or breaks down is to stay with the vehicle as they are always easier to see from the air than lone humans walking on a vast desert landscape.

People have died trying to walk long distances back to civilization because they were ill-prepared or succumbed to heat or cold. However, on occasion, the only way to survive is to walk out or walk to a highpoint to get cell phone reception, but you must be prepared. Each member of the Lawlor family has walked out at least once when their cars were stranded. They knew how far help was, they knew their abilities, the landscape, they had water, and were able make a good judgement call.

Getting your vehicle out is an entirely different story. Some back-country roads are more difficult to get out of than others. Don't expect the Auto Club to send up a 4-WD tow truck (they don't have any in their fleet). The tow companies in Vegas that advertise 4-WD vehicle recovery are expensive (about $1,000 minimum) and want to know that you have cash. The best club to hook up with is the Vegas Valley 4-Wheelers. They are a volunteer member organization who live for the challenge and love the backcountry. These are the best folks to ask. They are the most experienced four-wheel backcountry drivers in Clark County (and do accept donations for their Club).

Cell Phone Reception (or Lack Thereof)

Cell phone reception is completely non-existent is many back-country areas and most of Red Rock is no exception. There are major cell phone dead spots just three miles from Summerlin on SR-159 through Red Rock. Take a cell phone, but cell reception may not be available on most of the trails listed in this book.

Wilderness Sanitation

A large unsightly pile in the middle of the trail should be reason enough to want to dispose of the spoils your dog leaves behind, however there is a better reason: human and canine feces contaminate precious water sources. Red Rock is so popular with dog hikers, that complimentary waste bags are available at the trailheads. There are many products for scooping waste: plastic-baggy gloves, scoopers, zip-locks bags. Those plastic grocery and produce section bags also work well. On the trail, far from trash cans, loop a carabiner through a knot tied on a plastic bag and clip the bag to the outside of your daypack. Just be sure the grocery bags don't have any holes in them so they don't leak!

HEAT INJURY: HEAT EXHAUSTION AND HEAT STROKE

Every summer there is a new heat-related fatality reported on the local news. Heat will kill a dog as quickly as it will kill a human. On hot summer days my dog has no desire to leave the cool comfort of the air-conditioned house and she lets me know it (and I listen). The best way to avoid heat injury is to get an early in the morning start. While hiking, drink plenty of water. Pour spare water on your dog's head and back.

DANGER SIGNS IN HUMANS

Heat exhaustion in people and dogs is caused by a number of factors. Dehydration is caused by not drinking enough water to replenish what is lost through perspiration. Physical overexertion when it's too hot will also cause injury.

The temperature of a normal human body is 98.6 degrees. The slightest variation, even within two degrees up or down, reduces your physical and mental efficiency. The body absorbs heat from exposure to air and direct sunlight and by generating heat during physical exertion. If either is done too quickly, the body's core temperature is raised to excess, resulting in serious injury, even death.

Human symptoms of heat exhaustion include physical weakness, dizziness, nausea, vomiting and headache. If a hiking partner displays any of these symptoms, have them sit or lie down, preferably with feet elevated, in the shade. They must rest and drink water with an electrolyte additive until they are hydrated. Cool the skin down by patting the face and head with water.

Heat stroke is the complete failure of the body's temperature control systems. It can be fatal depending upon severity and treatment. Symptoms include confusion, agitation, hyperventilation, racing pulse, lethargy, convulsions, and eventually loss of consciousness. The body temperature rises to extremely high levels, sometimes above 110 degrees Fahrenheit. Such extremes can permanently damage major internal organs.

Avoid life threatening situations by knowing the danger signs of heat-related illnesses. Keep in mind that symptoms can develop over several days or strike during a single burst of strenuous activity. Two conditions, which signal that your body is under extreme stress from heat, are heat edema, and prickly heat.

Heat edema causes swelling of the hands and feet when blood vessels expand and allow fluid to pool under the skin. People often notice this first when their shoes feel too tight or one their rings won't fit the finger that they used to wear it on.

Prickly heat is an irritating rash that is caused by a blockage of the sweat pores, usually under clothing. This often happens when people overdress for the weather or wear clothing that is very fitted and doesn't "breathe." Neither of these conditions is harmful, but they are warning signs to cool off and avoid a more serious condition. Remove or loosen heavy and restrictive clothing, get out of the sun, and drink fluids immediately, preferably a sports drink like Gatorade.

Danger Signs in Dogs

Canine symptoms of heat exhaustion are like those experienced by humans: vomiting (especially after drinking), a stumbling gait, overall exhaustion, glassy or tired-looking eyes. Heat combined with dehydration and overexertion can have detrimental effects on a dog. Get the dog into shade and pat or pour water on his head, rub cool water into his coat to bring the body temperature down. Rest for as long as it takes.

When we first began hiking with our dogs in the Mojave Desert, our little cattle dog, Syd, was really out of shape. Along the trail, she ran for shade and started vomiting. By the time we got back to the car, she was completely exhausted, barely able to move: the result of heat, overexertion, dehydration and quite possibly a touch of altitude sickness. We opted for easier walks until she was in better condition, carried more water, stopped more often for water breaks and rubbed water on her head and along her back.

We sweat while dogs cool themselves by breathing, panting. A dog with a long snout can ventilate better than a dog with a short snout. Heat is especially dangerous for short-snouted dogs like pugs and boxers, older dogs, and dogs with heavy fur coats are more prone to the negative effects of heat.

Hypothermia

Hypothermia is the opposite of heat injury, but the ultimate physical effects are as serious. Ignoring the symptoms can cause death.

Exposure to cold and moisture causes the body's core temperature to drop to dangerous levels. This happens more frequently during the colder months but don't discount the possibility on the high trails and exposed ridges of the Spring Mountains during summer monsoon season. As the body experiences heat loss, from wearing wet clothes or not enough warm clothing in cold, windy, or wet conditions, the core temperature drops, impairing brain and muscular functions.

Danger Signs in Humans

Hypothermia's initial symptoms include chills and shivering, followed by numbness of the skin, muscular impairment, slow hand movement and increased difficulty talking. As the body temperature drops, the muscles become increasingly uncoordinated. There is a slowness of pace, mild confusion, apathy and amnesia. In severe cases, inability to walk or stand, confusion, dilation of pupils, unconsciousness and eventually death. To save a life, restore the body temperature with warm, dry clothes, quick energy food, and a "human sandwich"—wrap your warm body around the person inside a sleeping bag, preferably.

Preventing hypothermia requires adequate layered and rainproof clothing, food, and water. Drink liquids with an electrolyte additive or a sports drink to avoid dehydration. Eat snacks rich in carbs at frequent intervals to provide and restore energy for physical activity and the production of body heat.

Danger Signs in Dogs

Dogs experience uncontrollable shivering, weakness, difficulty moving, and a stumbling gait.

One of our dogs once broke through a snowbank and fell into the swift waters of Rock Creek in the Sierra Nevada. She was fully submerged and soaked when she clamored out downstream. A winter storm was coming in fast, dark gray clouds overhead and a very cold

Heading up Trail Canyon   PHOTO: Wynne Benti

wind blowing. By the time we got to the car, she was shivering uncontrollably. We wrapped her in a towel and turned the car heater on full blast, but she was still shivering. My husband got into the back of the car and held her, rubbing her down to warm her. With the warmth of a human body next to her and two big dog biscuits later, she finally stopped shivering.

DRESS IN LAYERS

Dressing in layers allows easy adjustment to changing outdoor temperature and precipitation. Cotton shorts and tee-shirts are great for summer hiking, but when cotton gets wet it takes forever to dry, trapping cold and moisture.

Dressing for survival is key in the Spring Mountains, even in the middle of summer. You can count on afternoon summer thunderstorms with huge temperature drops. Synthetic materials like polypro are the best insulators against cold and moisture, are lighter weight than wool, dry quickly if they get wet while retaining their insulating properties. Always carry a rain jacket and a lightweight pair of gloves. Add to that basic ensemble, rain pants, a lightweight polypro long-sleeve top and bottoms. That basic mountain fashion get-up could mean the difference between survival and not.

NATIVE SPECIES

In 1980, the population of Las Vegas was 400,000 and is just under two million in 2005. It is the most visited city in the United States second to Orlando, Florida. We've all seen and cried about the ever continuing expansion of development across the Las Vegas Valley. It has happened so fast over the past ten years, that entire localized habitats of native wildlife have been wiped out. Where you could once hear the coyotes at night, you can't hear them anymore. They are gone. Freeways and neighborhoods have pushed native species out into the desert forever. Those that adapted to the forced relocation survived, while others were not so lucky.

Precious water sources are gone, or have been locked in by concrete. Coyotes and other native species die just trying to cross roads to get a drink of water. Fires exacerbate the problem by destroying protective native scrub.

Encounters between people and native species, especially the larger ones–coyotes–will continue to occur. Give them respect. Be tolerant. Understand.

Leashes Help Protect Native Species

With ever-expanding development and human intrusion come domestic dogs. Benefiting from their close association with people and their genetic ties to wolves, domestic dogs unwittingly interfere with the habitat of native species by marking territory, sniffing burrows, chasing lizards and other animals. We can do our small part to help protect threatened native wildlife populations in the desert and mountain backcountry of Las Vegas by keeping our dogs under our control, by voice or leash, on and off the trails.

Rattlers, Burros and Other Desert Dwellers

Years ago, Megan and her husband Jeff were standing in their kitchen in what was downtown Las Vegas when a gila monster wandered into the house. Those were the good old days. The gila monsters are long gone from this area.

Rattlesnakes and burros are about the best reason we can think of to keep our dogs close. Rattlesnakes hibernate in winter, hide out in cool ledges, caves and rock shelters in summer (watch where you put your hands) and are out and about in spring and fall. 90% of snake bites to humans occur on the hands and below the knees. A rattlesnake bite can kill a dog. Access to medical attention must be immediate for humans and dogs. *Avoidance is the key.* There are canine classes on how to avoid rattlesnakes, but using the hands-free leashing method is the best defense!

Burros are a non-native species imported from the Middle East and brought west over a century ago as pack animals. They were turned loose or escaped into the southwest desert where they proliferated. Voracious grazers they competed with native species for precious grasses. Over the years, they have been removed from public lands through humane means and often, not so humane. The BLM has dedicated several areas to preserving the wild horse and burro populations of Nevada and California, and one of these is Red Rock.

Despite the signs warning not to do so, burros have been fed human food along Highway 159. As a result, they see humans as a food source. Burros will run after hikers for a handout. *Burros will aggressively chase and kill a dog thinking it a predator.* There have been several incidents in Red Rock where dogs have been seriously injured or killed by burros mistaking them for coyotes or wolves.

TICK CHECK

There are a few ticks here and there in the local mountains, but not much to worry about. In tick or mosquito heavy areas, a DEET-free insect repellent for humans can be used on dogs to minimize bites from ticks (Lyme disease) and mosquitoes (West Nile Virus). We have also sprayed Cutters on the dogs.

After every hike, give your dogs a full-body tick check. Run your hands through the fur, from the head to the end of tail. Ticks feel like small, protruding moles and measure from an 1/8" to 1/2" depending on how long they have been attached.

REMOVING A TICK

Use a pair of tweezers to remove a tick. Push the dog's fur away from the affected area. Place the tweezers closest to the point of tick contact with the dog, nearest to the tick's head (which is beneath the skin). Get a good firm grasp of the tick with the tweezers and pull it out with firm, dedicated force. Remove any leftover tick parts with the tweezers, then clean the affected area with soap and water. On the trail prepackaged alcohol pads are small, easy to carry and will clean both human and canine wounds. Contact your vet with any questions. Check yourself for ticks especially after hiking in terrain with brush and tall grass. It is quite disconcerting to find the little blood suckers in warm moist places!

MOSQUITOES

Luckily we don't have to worry much about ticks or mosquitoes in our arid climate. In mosquito country, they bite dogs and are a terrible nuisance. A mosquito swarming a dog will make that dog cry. To repel insects, use a DEET-free insect repellent like Natrapel. Spray directly or rub it on your hands then spread it over the dog's fur, head to tail, careful not to get it in their eyes.

Mountain Lions

We once saw two mountain lions on Turtlehead Peak. They were after bighorn sheep and quickly departed when we arrived. They are few and far between in our area, but they are out there.

Though your chance of being struck by lightning is greater than that of being attacked by a mountain lion or of winning the the Wheel of Fortune Jackpot, there are a few things to know! Mountain lions are primarily nocturnal, and survive primarily on smaller mammals, but will hunt deer and sheep. Attacks on humans are quick and usually come without warning, as lions ambush their prey from behind.

To minimize any encounters with lions, hike with a friend, a group, or your dog. Two moving objects are more intimidating than one. Studies have shown that mountain lions are especially attracted to children so keep small kids close to you. Never approach a lion. If you inadvertently meet up with one, give it a way to escape. Running from a mountain lion stimulates their instinct to chase. Try not to crouch or bend over (a person bending over or squatting looks like four-legged prey to a lion). Do all you can to appear larger; remain standing, raise your arms and wave them slowly while speaking in a firm, loud voice; throw stones, branches, whatever you get in your hands without turning your back or bending over. Fight back if attacked—remain standing and face the lion. People have fought mountain lions off successfully using rocks, sticks, garden tools, jackets and bare hands.

Cholla Balls

Chollas have nasty barbed spines that lock into skin and are impossible to remove by hand. Needle nose pliers or tweezers are a must-have for removing jumping cholla and cactus spines from dog paws. If neither of those tools are handy, remove the chollas with two rocks. Do not use bare fingers. Our dogs are so familiar with cholla balls, that if one gets imbedded in a paw, they stop, hold up their paw and wait for removal.

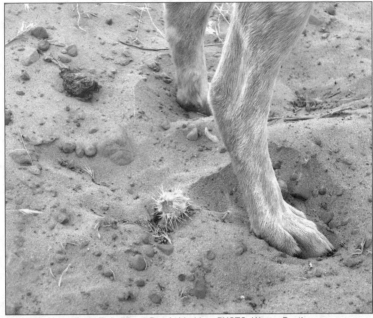
A cholla ball near Rosy's hind leg PHOTO: Wynne Benti

HEADING OUT

Let someone know where you are going and when you will be back and who to call if you don't show. Once you get stranded, it's really hard to call anyone! Here are a few items we include in our daypack:

1. Map
2. Headlamp, spare batteries
3. Water/food (minimum 2.5 gallons spare water in the car)
4. Clothing (lightweight raingear and long underwear)
5. Pocket knife
6. Matches
7. Hat, sun glasses, sunscreen
8. Cell phone (reception on high points but not in most canyons)
9. First aid kit (tweezers, neosporine, bandages, waterproof tape)
10. Space blanket

MANY OF THE TRAILS LISTED IN THIS BOOK ARE WATERLESS! WATER (WITH EXTRA IN THE CAR) IS THE MOST IMPORTANT ITEM YOU CAN CARRY, THE DIFFERENCE BETWEEN LIFE OR DEATH.

DOGS:

1. Water (two-liter soda bottles work great)
2. Bowl
3. ID tag, implanted pet recovery chip
4. Leash
5. Zip-lock with snacks and/or dry dog food

IN THE CAR:

1. Minimum one-gallon jug of spare water wrapped in a sleeping bag for insulation or kept in a cooler
2. Bowl
3. Paper towels and plastic bags (for car sickness or other accidents)

COMFORTABLE HIKING OR WALKING SHOES

A pair of comfortable hiking boots with good soles is essential. Walking for miles on blistered heels is a miserable experience. Dog paws are also sensitive to rough terrain. Sore, cut, or worn-out paw pads are probably the most common reasons for having to carry a dog out of the backcountry. The Bonzana King limestone formation of the Las Madres is especially hard on dog paws.

Making a set of dog boots using the pattern provided in this book is a good way to avoid this problem. You can try dog packs on day-hikes. Dogs have more fun without them. Padded dog packs are better for overnight trips where a couple of days will make a difference in the amount of weight carried.

DOG HIKING BOOTS

The best canine hiking boots are made from soft, pliable leather or suede. Following years of experimentation fellow K9 hiker, Terry Austin, discovered that he could make boots with relative ease for his Golden Retriever, Tama. Using suede, shoelaces and two simple tools, the boots Terry designed for Tama were a very practical solution for protecting his paws on rugged terrain or on long hikes.

Using the basic pattern shown on the following pages (final size will vary depending on the size of your dog's paws), a set of four suede booties with spares, can be easily made for a reasonable cost. When you are ready to make the boots, first size your dog's paws with a sample boot pattern cut from paper or cloth. This way, you

should be able to get an exact fit without expending any of your real materials. Nylon shoelaces are durable and seem to be the best material for longevity. They must be tied securely around the paws so the boots do not slip or fall off.

Initially your dog will probably walk funny, picking up each paw in a curious high-step gait but as they get used to wearing their boots, they'll learn to walk normally!

Dog boot designer Terry Austin puts on Tama's boots, while Tama relaxes just before the hike.

HOW TO MAKE YOUR OWN DOG HIKING BOOTS

MATERIALS NEEDED:
GOOD QUALITY SUEDE LEATHER
A HOLE-PUNCHING TOOL
AN EYE-RIVETING TOOL
27" NYLON SHOELACES
OUR PATTERN AS SHOWN ON THE FOLLOWING PAGES

USING THE PATTERN ON THE NEXT TWO PAGES, CUT SAMPLES OUT OF PAPER OR FABRIC TO DETERMINE SIZING FOR ALL FOUR PAWS. TRACE THE PATTERN ONTO LEATHER USING A LIGHT COLOR PENCIL. CUT THE BOOT SHAPE OUT OF THE LEATHER. PUNCH HOLES FOR LACES, FRONT CLAWS. RIVET HOLES FOR LACES ONLY. LACE SHOELACES (USE DIFFERENT COLORS FOR A STYLISH LOOK) THROUGH HOLES, AND PRESTO! A NEW SET OF FINE HIKING BOOTS FOR YOUR CANINE COMPANION!

TERRY AUSTIN'S PATTERN FOR DOG HIKING BOOTS

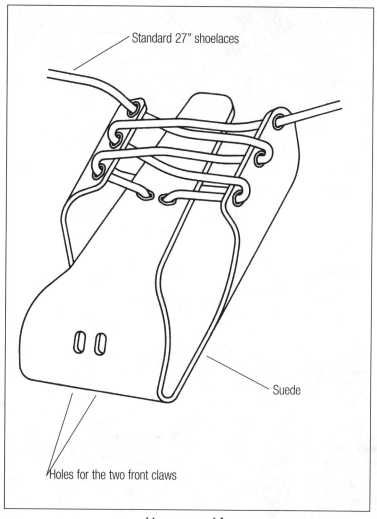

Standard 27" shoelaces

Suede

Holes for the two front claws

MATERIALS NEEDED

GOOD QUALITY SUEDE LEATHER, A HOLE-PUNCHING TOOL,
AN EYE-RIVETING TOOL AND 27" NYLON SHOELACES.

DIMENSIONS SHOWN ON THESE PAGES ARE FOR LARGER DOGS.
CUSTOMIZE LENGTHS AND WIDTHS TO FIT YOUR DOG'S PAWS.
DRAWINGS SHOWN ARE NOT TO SIZE.

CANINE BOOT DESIGN AND DRAWINGS BY TERRY AUSTIN ©1995-2006

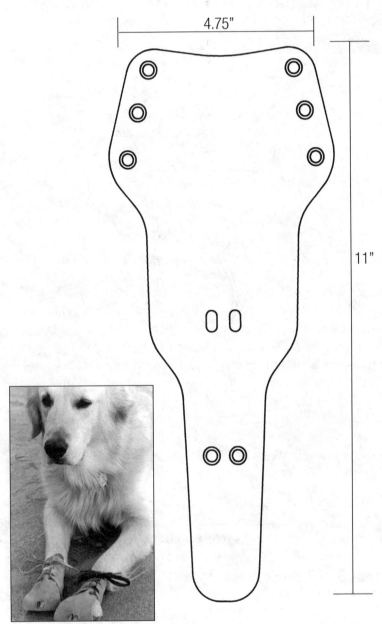

4.75"

11"

Tama models his boots PHOTO: Terry Austin

Contemplating the "no pets" sign
PHOTO: Julie Rush

MAPS

Directions to trailheads, driving instructions and maps for each hike in this book are listed at the top of each hike description. For most of the drives listed in the book, a AAA map or the Nevada Road & Recreation Atlas by Benchmark Maps will work.

Topographic maps (topos) are surveyed and drawn by the United States Geographical Survey, the USGS. In the not so distant past, one could readily buy USGS 15-minute (minute refers to latitude and longitude) maps that displayed a much larger area, but those have been phased out in favor of the more detailed 7.5-minute maps or quadrangles (quads) that show half the area of the old maps. Most topos are available online or at local outdoor equipment supply or travel stores like *Gotta Get A Map* in downtown Las Vegas. Older topos show only the geographical details not the trails, since most of the trails were constructed after the areas were surveyed and the maps printed.

The *Green Trails Map of Red Rock Canyon National Conservation Area* is highly recommended for Red Rock. As of press time, their cartographer told us they are working on one for the Spring Mountains. In the meantime, the USGS Las Vegas 1:100 000-scale metric topo map is a good overall map for the central Spring Mountains.

TRAIL ACCESS

Each government agency, city, county, state or federal, that oversees public park lands, has its own set of rules concerning dogs, including but not limited to the use of leashes, owner control and access. Regulations are usually posted at the trailhead or available from the park agency.

There is nothing more frustrating then getting up at o'dark-thirty to pack for a full-day's excursion with your dog, drive an hour or

Rosy and Jim on the summit of Mummy Mountain PHOTO: Wynne Benti

more to a trailhead, only to discover a trail or road closure. It pays to call ahead if you're unsure about the regulations concerning dogs.

All owners are responsible for their dog's behavior on the trail and for knowing all the rules that apply to dogs for the particular area they'll be visiting.

CAR TRAVELING WITH YOUR DOG

Here a few helpful tips for traveling with your dog.

• Water and lightly feed your dog before leaving

• Keep a water bowl, partially filled, in a flat spot in the car so the dog can drink as needed

• Bring a padded blanket or dog bed for extra comfort

• Dogs do get car sick (both ends!)—carry paper towels and plastic bags for cleaning up accidents

• If your dog must smell the fresh air, keep the window open enough that they can just get their noses out. A dog standing in an open car window could fall out of the window on a bump, corner or quick stop.

• Lock all power windows while traveling. A dog can step on the power switch, roll up the window catching their head in the closed window with body dangling. Or, they might roll the window down and fall out. A horrifying experience either way.

• Don't leave the keys in the car with the dog and the engine running! Wynne did this once and Rosy locked her out of the car by scratching on the windows and inadvertently hitting the power door lock button. Luckily ten minutes later Rosy, unlocked the doors.

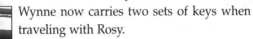

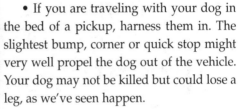

Wynne now carries two sets of keys when traveling with Rosy.

• If you are traveling with your dog in the bed of a pickup, harness them in. The slightest bump, corner or quick stop might very well propel the dog out of the vehicle. Your dog may not be killed but could lose a leg, as we've seen happen.

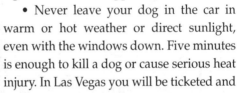

• Never leave your dog in the car in warm or hot weather or direct sunlight, even with the windows down. Five minutes is enough to kill a dog or cause serious heat injury. In Las Vegas you will be ticketed and

prosecuted, depending on the severity of the offense, if you leave a dog or child in a hot car.

RATING THE HIKES FOR DIFFICULTY

Listed in the hike headings are the minimum water requirements for a medium-sized dog, based on moderate desert temperatures. With the exception of some slippery steep scrambling on Mummy Mountain, technical skill for dog or owner is not necessary on the hikes in this book. Just a healthy set of lungs and the desire to have a wonderful time are all that's required. Ratings of difficulty are based on mileage, elevation gain and dog abilities and are as follows:

Easy: Good hikes for dogs and people just starting out on the trail, older dogs, small dogs, out-of-shape dogs and people looking for some weekend exercise, or who are getting into shape for more challenging trips.

Moderate: Dogs and people need to be in good physical condition, walking two to three times a week, a total of three to five miles.

Strenuous: Dogs and people should be experienced hikers, in excellent physical condition with a weekly exercise routine that includes six to ten miles per week with hill climbing.

The more you hike with your dog, the easier it will be to judge her hiking ability, skill level and water needs (two quarts minimum *just for your dog*).

RATING THE HIKES FOR DIFFICULTY

SUPER EASY ALL DOGS AND PEOPLE JUST STARTING OUT, FROM THE ELDERLY, OUT-OF-SHAPE TO THE VERY SMALL DOG. NO EXPERIENCE REQUIRED.

EASY ALL DOGS AND PEOPLE FROM THE ELDERLY, OUT-OF-SHAPE TO THE VERY SMALL DOG WHO ARE OUT WALKING EVERY COUPLE OF DAYS.

MODERATE DOGS AND PEOPLE SHOULD BE TAKING LONG DAILY WALKS, A TOTAL OF TWO-FOUR MILES PER WEEK WITH SOME UP AND DOWNS.

STRENUOUS DOGS AND PEOPLE SHOULD BE EXPERIENCED HIKERS, IN EXCELLENT PHYSICAL CONDITION WITH A WEEKLY EXERCISE ROUTINE THAT INCLUDES 4-6 MILES PER WEEK WITH HILL CLIMBING OR UPS AND DOWNS.

DIFFICULT REQUIRES SPECIAL SKILLS SUCH AS MAP-READING, ROUTE-FINDING, CROSS-COUNTRY TRAVEL, BEING ABLE TO LOOK AT THE IMMEDIATE TERRAIN AND SELECT A SAFE DOABLE PATH THROUGH OBSTACLES. SKILL WILL BE LISTED IN HIKE HEADING.

THE SPRING MOUNTAINS

The most extensive and tallest of Nevada's southern ranges, the fabulous Spring Mountains, 316,000 acres within the Humboldt-Toiyabe National Forest, offer an alpine summer oasis less than an hour's drive (depending on traffic) from downtown Las Vegas. While the immediate surrounding environs bake in the hot desert sun, there are a myriad of pleasant, cool hikes to high altitudes or hidden canyons with a surprising amount of water almost year-round. In fact, the summer of 2005 saw up to thirty-feet of leftover winter snow in some canyons at the beginning of August! Charleston Peak (11,915') is the high point of the range and the eighth highest peak in the state. Mummy Mountain at (11,530') was named for its remarkable similarity to an outstretched Egyptian mummy.

WEATHER

The Spring Mountains make their own weather and it's not uncommon to start hiking early on a summer morning with clear blue skies and by early-afternoon be caught in a torrential downpour complete with lightening, thunder and hail. Up on the high ridges of the Spring Mountains the temperature can be up to thirty-degrees cooler in summer than in Las Vegas. That's a big difference. It's best to plan starting long hikes in early morning.

Always carry plenty of water at least 2-liters minimum (the size of one large soda bottle) for your dog. Autumn, winter and spring are best for hiking the more demanding trails. Daytime temperatures can easily climb over eighty degrees any time of the year. There is no shade on many of the trails.

Check the weather report prior to your hike. Afternoon thunderstorms are typical of the summer monsoon season. Leave early enough to make sure you are off the higher, exposed summit ridges before the afternoon thunderstorms. The summits of almost all the main peaks are above treeline and afford no protection from lightning. Once, just below Charleston Peak's summit, we saw lightning bolts striking the metal posts on either side of the summit register.

GEOLOGY

Mt. Stirling and McFarland to the north are typical of the single-ridged north-south trending ranges common to the Great Basin. Charleston Peak and Mummy Mountain to the south are more massive then those peaks to the north. The La Madre Mountain-Sandstone Bluffs portion of the look like a combination of the jagged Dolomites and the red sandstone of Zion. Potosi Mountain, across from Mountain Springs Summit is a great dome. In the canyons on the way to the peak, one can see remnants of the ancient warm seas trapped in the limestone rock: ferns, reeds, shells. Potosi Mountain is best known perhaps as that which claimed the life of Clark Gable's love, actress Carole Lombard, when the plane she was riding in, along with twenty-one other passengers and crew, crashed.

Perhaps the most striking and unique geologic features of the Spring Mountains are the thrust faults. Oriented at low angles, thrust faults occur where the land has been squeezed together, forcing one group of rocks to ride atop another. These phenomena result in older rocks lying on top of younger rocks, just the opposite of what would be the logical progression.

The most striking of the thrust faults in the area is the Keystone Thrust which places much older, Cambrian-age Bonzana King Formation limestones on top of the striking white and red Aztec Sandstone that inspired the naming of Red Rock National

The USFS Fulton Hotshots helicopter crash in the Spring Mountains PHOTO: Mike Farrell

Conservation Area. When climbing the peaks of the Sandstone Bluffs (Bridge, Rainbow, Wilson) or Turtlehead Peak, the climber will pass over the trace of this fantastic structure.

FIRE

Over the years, fires, man-made and natural, have swept across the Spring Mountains killing wildlife, destroying vegetation. It takes years for the land to recover from these fires. During periods of great fire hazard, the USFS will post fire closures at road access points to the Spring Mountains and on their website at:

http://www.fs.fed.us/r4/htnf/districts/smnra.shtml

One friend of ours, a firefighter with the USFS Fulton Hotshots out of Sequoia National Forest was flown in from California to fight a major fire in the Spring Mountains in the 1980s. These men and women put their lives at risk every time they head into the back-country to subdue a man-made fire and that trip was no exception.

The firefighter recalled, "We were coming down fast on the top of a mountain. When we saw a crewman on the ground start running, we knew something was wrong." Their helicopter came in too hard on the summit of one of the peaks, and rolled down the mountainside (pictured above). Luckily all survived the crash.

Megan on the Cathedral Rock trail PHOTO: Wynne Benti

FLORA

More than 1,000 species of plants have been recorded within the Spring Mountains, a fairly impressive number. The exposed summit of Charleston Peak, constantly battered by lightning, hail, rain, intense wind, snow and UV, is fairly devoid of any plant life. This bleak picture of a classic, above-timberline peak is in complete contrast to the treeline merely a hundred feet below the summit where bristlecone pines and limber pines provide excellent photographic opportunities.

Below the bristlecones, a mixed forest of aspen, white fir, and ponderosa pine are found. These trees are common in the Charleston-Mummy region. However, a few pines and firs can also be found on the slopes of Potosi and La Madre Mountain. Beneath this pine-fir-aspen forest, the pinyon-juniper woodlands become prominent, giving way to sagebrush scrub with scattered Joshua trees and yuccas on the lower slopes. In the lower mountains south of Potosi (below about 4,000 feet) creosote becomes dominant.

FAUNA

Among the animals known to occur within the Spring Mountains are coyote, elk, porcupine, bobcat, mule deer, bighorn sheep, badger, gray fox and a host of smaller mammals. The reptiles are also very diverse here: desert iguanas, geckos, whiptails, collard, horned, fence, and leopard lizards just to name a few. The Mojave Desert sidewinder, Panamint rattlesnake, desert glossy snake, Mojave shovel-nosed snake, king snakes, night snakes, and gopher snakes are just a few of the many snakes that have carved out their niche in the Spring Mountains. Keep an eye out for these mountain inhabitants during your excursions.

PICNIC AREAS

There are several fine picnic areas in the Spring Mountains where dogs are welcome on leash:

CATHEDRAL ROCK (7,600')

From Las Vegas take US-95 north to SR-157/Kyle Canyon and turn left. Drive 21 miles to the end of the road and the entrance.

DEER CREEK (8,200')

From Las Vegas take US-95 north to SR-157/Kyle Canyon and turn left

At Mazie Spring PHOTO: Wynne Benti

and drive 17 miles to SR-158 (to Lee Canyon). Turn right and drive about 4.0 miles to the entrance.

FOXTAIL (8,300')

From Las Vegas take US-95 north to SR-156/Lee Canyon. Turn left and drive 16 miles to the picnic area.

OLD MILL (8,300')

From Las Vegas take US-95 north to SR-156/Lee Canyon. Turn left and drive 16 miles to the picnic area.

CAMPING

Camping is available in several campgrounds throughout the range. Supplies, gas, food and lodging are available in Las Vegas. Fine lodging and dining are also available at the Mt. Charleston Hotel in Kyle Canyon.

For further information on the portion of the Spring Mountains from Mount Stirling to Harris Mountain, contact the Toiyabe National Forest-Spring Mountain National Recreation Area office in Las Vegas.

For information on the La Madre Mountain/Sandstone Bluffs area, contact the Red Rock National Conservation Area. Information for the area south of Mountain Springs Summit, can be obtained from the Bureau of Land Management office in Las Vegas.

KYLE CANYON AND VICINITY
FLETCHER CANYON

Rating: Easy
Recommended for: Small, out-of-shape or older dogs
Round-trip mileage: 3.8 miles, 2-3 hours
K9 water: Water; 1-quart minimum
Posted: Pets on leash. Clean up after your pet
Ambience: Lots of shade with a unique box canyon at end
Best time to hike: April to November

Driving

Maps: Nevada Road & Recreation Atlas, AAA Las Vegas Vicinity Guide

From the junction of I-15 and US-95, take US-95 north to SR-157/Kyle Canyon and turn left, west, and drive approximately 17.7 miles to the signed Fletcher Canyon trailhead, about 0.5 miles past SR-158 to Lee Canyon. There is parking at the trailhead and across the street. Before leaving the car make sure your dog is on leash as the parking area is at the edge of a busy road, especially on weekends.

Hiking

Map: USGS Angel Peak (NV) 7.5-Minute (1:24,000 scale) Quad

The Fletcher Canyon Trail is easy to follow as it parallels a dry creek bed. When we visited here in August, surprisingly, the creek was not dry. On a wet year with a lot of snow melt, expect flowing water in this canyon. The forest of mountain mahogany, pinyon and ponderosa pine shade the meandering trail. Ponderosa is the tallest pine in the Spring Mountains, growing up to 150 feet and living as long as 500 years. Native Americans gathered the seeds of the pinyon pine and ate them raw or ground them up to make bread. A variety of small mammals and birds rely on the seeds of the pinyon for food.

Fletcher Canyon PHOTO: Megan Lawlor

About forty minutes into the hike and deeper into the canyon, the trail narrows. The vegetation becomes increasingly beautiful—a lush wonderland of Queen Anne's lace flowers growing as high as eight feet, wild roses, small dainty columbine and blueberry elder. To the right along the spring as you head into the slot canyon notice a large impressive cave-like arch. The stunning limestone cliffs, trickling with water, create quite an intimate setting as they soar to heights over one hundred feet. Just a little further up this narrow part of the canyon is a dead end—or is it? This geological anomaly is called Obstacle Rock, and we make it the end of our hike. Hiking beyond this rock will put you out on the North Loop Trail.

Notes

As with any narrow canyon do not enter if rain is predicted!

Cathedral Rock

Rating: Moderate
Recommended for: Well-conditioned dogs, any size
Round-trip mileage: 2.4 miles, 955' gain, 2-3 hours
K9 water: Water; 2-quart minimum
Posted: Pets on leash. Clean up after your pet
Ambience: Meandering trail through manzanita, pinyon, ponderosa
Best time to hike: April to November

Driving

Maps: Nevada Road & Recreation Atlas, AAA Las Vegas Vicinity Guide

From the junction of I-15 and US-95, take US-95 north to SR-157/Kyle Canyon and turn left, west. At approximately 20 miles, stay left on

Rosy on the Cathedral Rock Trail PHOTO: Wynne Benti

SR-157 at a sharp curve also the junction with Echo Road, about 0.5 miles past the Mt. Charleston fire station.

Drive another 0.4 miles to the free parking area on the right (restrooms). If this lot is full, there is additional parking along the street and up in the picnic area (fee).

Hiking

Map: USGS Charleston Peak (NV) 7.5-Minute (1:24,000 scale) Quad

From the parking lot walk up the steps to the signed Cathedral Rock Trail and turn left. Follow trail through forest, then east across what is now a major debris field. The trail was obliterated by an avalanche during the winter of 2004 prompting USFS trail crews to work furiously throughout 2005 to get the trail cleared of debris.

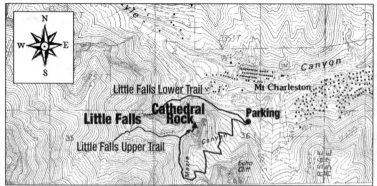
Cathedral Rock and upper and lower trails to Little Falls PHOTO: Megan Lawlor

About forty minutes into the hike, there is a cool snowed spring off the trail to the left, the outflow of Mazie Spring, a wonderful spot to cool off. Small orange columbine and wild roses bloom along its flanks during early summer.

Continue on the main trail, which leaves the avalanche path and meanders through the pines. This part of the trail is pleasantly level and delightfully shady. At the next trail fork at the saddle below Cathedral Rock, take the right fork passing a creek. The left fork goes an additional 0.5 miles to Little Falls overlook and continues on about 0.2 miles past that point (about 780' gain from the saddle to trail end).

Follow several tight, spiraling switchbacks to the peak where views of the entire canyon and lodge below are spectacular. There are no barriers at the top so keep dogs leashed and several feet back from the edge where sheer cliffs drop one hundred feet or more.

Notes

Cathedral Rock is one of Mt. Charleston's most popular trails, and has long been a favorite of ours. It has all the rewards of a long hike without the work. From the summit atop Kyle Canyon, the panoramic views are marvelous. In autumn, the aspen leaves turn yellow, then deep orange and red before covering the ground in a multi-colored blanket. In late spring and summer, spectacular displays of blue purple lupine grow densely along the trail. Graceful looking Queen Anne's lace makes an appearance along the trail while butterflies flutter in and out like magical fairies.

Little Falls

Rating: Moderate
Recommended for: Well-conditioned dogs, any size
Round-trip mileage: 1.4 miles, 400' gain, 1-1.5 hours
K9 water: Water; 2-quart minimum
Posted: Pets on leash. Clean up after your pet
Ambience: Meandering trail through manzanita, pinyon, ponderosa
Best time to hike: April to November

Driving

Maps: Nevada Road & Recreation Atlas, AAA Las Vegas Vicinity Guide

From the junction of I-15 and US-95, take US-95 north to SR-157/Kyle Canyon and turn left, west. At approximately 20 miles, stay left on SR-157 at a sharp curve also the junction with Echo Road, about 0.5 miles past the Mt. Charleston fire station.

Drive another 0.4 miles to the free parking area on the right (restrooms). If this lot is full, there is additional parking along the street and up in the picnic area (fee).

Hiking

Map: USGS Charleston Peak (NV) 7.5-Minute (1:24,000 scale) Quad

From the parking lot walk up the steps to the signed Cathedral Rock Trail and turn right to Little Falls. We call this the lower trail because it puts you under the waterfall. Follow the path as it parallels the road below to the next narrow canyon on the left (the signed washed out during the 2004-2005 winter). Turn left up the canyon. Pick your way through the avalanche debris, on and off, the trail to the base of the falls.

Alternate Hiking Route from Cathedral Rock

Read the trail instructions in the previous description for Cathedral Rock. At the fork below the final switchbacks to Cathedral Rock's summit, take the left fork and additional 0.5 mile to an overlook of Little Falls, the upper trail. The trail continues another 0.2 mile more. About 780' gain.

MARY JANE FALLS

Rating: Moderate
Recommended for: Well-conditioned dogs, any size
Round-trip mileage: 3.0 miles, 820' gain, 1.5-2 hours
K9 water: Seasonal water at falls; 1-quart minimum
Posted: Pets on leash. Clean up after your pet.
Ambience: Hike through the pines to waterfall
Best time to hike: April to November

Driving

Maps: Nevada Road & Recreation Atlas, AAA Las Vegas Vicinity Guide

From the junction of I-15 and US-95, take US-95 north to SR-157/Kyle Canyon and turn left, west. At 20 miles, bear right (or straight ahead) on Echo Road (about 0.5 miles past the Mt. Charleston fire station) SR-157 curves sharp left at this intersection. At 20.4 mile bear left at a fork on a gravel road. At 20.6 reach the parking lot and trailhead for Mary Jane Falls. This is also the trailhead for Big Falls and Hidden Falls.

Hiking

Map: USGS Charleston Peak (NV) 7.5-Minute (1:24,000 scale) Quad

The signed trail begins at the north end of the parking lot next to the interpretive sign. Follow this wide trail about a half mile to a fork and bear right (the left fork goes to Big Falls).

The trail narrows from a road to a footpath. You gain elevation quickly on the steepening trail and switchbacks. After about a half an hour up the trail you will come to the switchbacks that traverse up the East side. The scenery is lovely along the way. Soon you will come to some stone steps and after making your way up these, the falls are minutes away.At the top of the falls, if you look to your west you will be able to see Big Falls. More advanced climbers have taken to climbing above Big Falls to reach Charleston's Summit. A few were stranded and rescued by helicopter. As you cool off at the falls notice a cave to the left of them. The roof is not fire blackened, which might indicate previous inhabitants. It's nice to imagine someone enjoying the shelter and cool mist from the falls. The area at the base of the falls is quite large and a great place to have lunch, so pack some goodies.

At Mary Jane Falls PHOTO: Megan Lawlor

Notes

The trail is well maintained and very popular on the weekends.

According to information in Volume 4 of the Mt. Charleston History, Mary Jane Falls was named after Mary Jane Reiter, a lifelong Las Vegan and daughter of Nevada pioneer Robert B. Griffith for whom Griffith Peak is named.

In the mid 1960s, the area above the parking lot where the trails traverse was once a popular picnic area that we visited many times as children. The remnants of concrete foundations can still be seen in some places. 1969 was a year of record snow at Kyle Canyon and five avalanches roared through the picnic area, destroying everything. A woman and her nine year old son were killed when it crashed into their home sweeping it down the mountainside. An eighteen-month old girl survived as she rode out the disaster protected in her crib!

BIG FALLS

Rating: Moderate
Recommended for: Well-conditioned dogs, any size
Round-trip mileage: 4.0 miles, 990' gain, 2-3 hours
K9 water: Seasonal water in creek; 2-quart minimum
Posted: Pets on leash. Clean up after your pet.
Ambience: Navigate a boulder-strewn creek to the falls
Best time to hike: April to November

Driving
Map: Nevada Road & Recreation Atlas, AAA Las Vegas Vicinity Guide
Same as Mary Jane Falls.

Hiking
Maps: Nevada Road & Recreation Atlas, AAA Las Vegas Vicinity Guide

The signed trail begins at the north end of the parking lot next to the interpretive sign. Follow this wide old Jeep trail just over a half mile to a fork and bear left. Continue left on the dirt trail as it merges with a well-worn foot trail that drops down into the boulder-strewn creek in the main canyon. Turn right, south, up the creek (so to speak!). Follow the creek back and forth, cross-country, as it climbs up into canyon. Higher up at the head of the avalanche debris field (and/or snow field depending on the year), a narrow, steep use trail climbs up on the left, east, side of the canyon above the snow field. Eventually the use-trail drops you back down on the debris field at the foot of Big Falls. Most people brave the slippery snowfield using a walking stick for better support. Above you is

August snowbank at Big Falls
PHOTO: Wynne Benti

Charleston Peak and in fact for experienced hikers, this is the fastest,

Beautiful Big Falls in late August after a heavy winter PHOTO: Wynne Benti

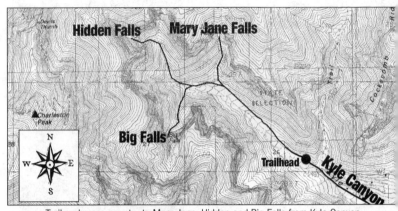

Trail and cross-country to Mary Jane, Hidden and Big Falls from Kyle Canyon

yet steepest way up to Charleston. Inexperienced folk have been air-lifted off the rocky slopes from time to time.

Notes

On November 17, 1955, a C-54 left the Lockheed's *Skunk Works* in Burbank, California, for Groom Lake—Area 51. Blown off course by

a severe storm, the plane crashed near the summit of Charleston Peak killing four crewmen and ten civilians. Because the mission was classified, Kyle Canyon was closed. A press release was issued that the downed plane was on a routine business trip to Indian Springs. In 2001, a resolution was presented by the Nevada State Legislature urging Congress to declare the 1955 crash site of the United States Air Force C54 near the summit of Mount Charleston as the "Silent Heroes of the Cold War National Monument." Wreckage from that crash can still be found in Big Falls Canyon.

Hidden Falls

Rating: Moderately-strenuous
Recommended for: Well-conditioned dogs, any size
Round-trip mileage: 3.0 miles, 1080' gain, 2-3 hours
K9 water: Seasonal water in creek; 2-quart minimum
Posted: Pets on leash. Clean up after your pet.
Ambience: Most rugged of the three waterfall hikes, wander the canyon to a steep-walled chasm along the base of Charleston Peak
Best time to hike: April to November

Driving
Maps: Nevada Road & Recreation Atlas, AAA Las Vegas Vicinity Guide
Same as Mary Jane Falls.

Hiking
Map: USGS Charleston Peak (NV) 7.5-Minute (1:24,000 scale) Quad
The signed trail begins at the north end of the parking lot to the right of the interpretive sign. Follow this wide old Jeep trail just over a half mile to a fork and bear left. Continue left on the dirt trail. Before the trail begins to drop down into the Big Falls drainage, turn right up the wide canyon to the north.

When we scouted this in August 2005, it was full of snow covered by a very thick blanket of avalanche debris–broken tree branches, pine cones and needles. The walking wasn't the easiest. Drier years make for much easier walking and boulder-hopping up the canyon bottom. The canyon is beautiful on a summer's day.

About 0.2 of mile up the canyon, pass a minor drainage on the left, staying in the main canyon. About 0.3 mile up, the canyon forks, bear left. Circuitous steep walls Follow the canyon as it narrows to the seasonal falls. Heavy winters promise good waterfalls throughout the summer. Return the same way.

CAVE SPRING VIA TRAIL CANYON

Rating: Moderate
Recommended for: Well-conditioned dogs, any size
Round-trip mileage: 5.2 miles, 2,135' gain, 3-4 hours
K9 water: Water at spring; 2-quart minimum
Posted: Pets on leash. Clean up after your pet.
Ambience: Steep trail through forest and bristlecone to quiet trailside spring
Best time to hike: April to December (depending on snow)

Driving
Maps: Nevada Road & Recreation Atlas, AAA Las Vegas Vicinity Guide
From the junction of I-15 and US-95, take US-95 north to Hwy. 157-Kyle Canyon and turn left, west). At 20 miles, turn right on Echo Road (about 0.5 miles past the Mt. Charleston fire station). Hwy. 157 curves sharp left at this intersection. About a half mile further is the Trail Canyon trailhead, at the intersection of Echo Road and Crestview. Park along the roadway. At press time, Las Vegas Valley Water District had closed the road just past the intersection of Echo and 157, while building a new water storage tank on top of the old trailhead. The trailhead was rerouted about 50 feet below the old.

Hiking
Map: USGS Charleston Peak (NV) 7.5-Minute (1:24,000 scale) Quad
Just follow the trail up the canyon. A short wa y up the trail and to the left you may notice small caves. To the right is Cockscomb Ridge, so named because the rocks jutting out appear to resemble a rooster's head. Two miles to its intersection with the North Loop Trail. Turn left and hike an additional 0.5 mile to Cave Spring with its lovely water trough.

Notes
Trail Canyon is a popular starting point for hikers wishing to climb Charleston Peak. Rock climbers use it to access "The Hood," a rock-climbing area in the steep overhanging limestone cliffs off to the left.

Most of the trail is exposed and can be hot in the summer, however there are many shady spots to rest. Bordered patch butterflies, black with rows of white dots, flutter amongst vibrant yellow desert daisies,

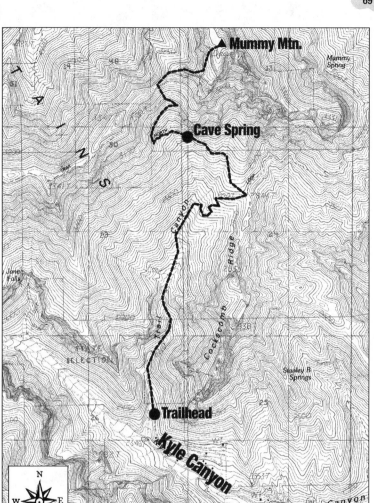

Trail to Mummy Mountain from Trail Canyon

red sky rockets, and Indian paintbrush. The musk thistle, *Carduus nutansm*, a European native introduced as an ornamental in the 19th century, stands two to four feet with beautiful pink flowers that attract large moths. Unfortunately, the musk thistle, an inedible pest weed is best known for invading and destroying western rangelands.

Two happy dogs at Cave Springs PHOTO: Wynne Benti

MUMMY MOUNTAIN (11,528 ft; 3,513.7 m)
VIA TRAIL CANYON

Rating: Strenuous, off-route Class 2 scrambling on loose scree
and a narrow ridge
Recommended for: Well-conditioned dogs, medium-sized and above
Round-trip mileage: 8.0 miles, 3,820' gain, 6-7 hours
K9 water: Water at spring; 2-quart minimum
Posted: Pets on leash. Clean up after your pet.
Ambience: Steep route via trail and cross-country with spectacular vistas
Best time to hike: April to November

Driving
Maps: Nevada Road & Recreation Atlas, AAA Las Vegas Vicinity Guide
From the junction of I-15 and US-95, take US-95 north to SR-157/Kyle
Canyon and turn left, west. At 20 miles, turn right on Echo Road
(about 0.5 miles past the Mt. Charleston fire station). SR-157 curves
sharp left at this intersection. About a half mile further is the Trail
Canyon trailhead, at the intersection of Echo Road and Crestview.
Park along the roadway.

At press time, Las Vegas Valley Water District had closed the road
just past the intersection of Echo and 157, while building a new water
storage tank on top of the old trailhead. The trailhead was rerouted
about fifty feet below the old.

Hiking
Map: USGS Charleston Peak (NV) 7.5-Minute (1:24,000 scale) Quad
Just follow the trail up the canyon 2.0 miles to its intersection with the
North Loop Trail. Turn left and hike another 0.75 mile to a very steep,
loose scree slope on the north side of the trail. Across from this spot
where you turn right to climb the scree slope, someone carved an
arrow in the tree on the south side of the trail, opposite the slope.

The scree slope is followed to a shallow saddle just west of the
base of the narrow north-south trending ridge to the summit massif.
This is followed (watch the sheer drop-offs on the right east, side) to
a narrow loose chute, the only opening in what appears to be a rock
wall, leads to the summit of Mummy. The register is in a rock cairn
east from the top of the chute.

Heading up the scree slope from Trail Canyon to Mummy   PHOTO: Wynne Benti

CHARLESTON PEAK (11,915 ft; 3631.7 m) VIA SOUTH LOOP TRAIL

Rating: Very strenuous!
Recommended for: Well-conditioned dogs only!
Round-trip mileage: 18 miles, 4,300' gain, 2-3 hours
K9 water: Seasonal water at falls; 1-quart minimum
Posted: Pets on leash. Clean up after your pet.
Ambience: Strenuously long route from piny forest to above-timberline
Best time to hike: April to November
Alternate Routes: North Loop Trail, Lee Canyon

Driving

Maps: Nevada Road & Recreation Atlas, AAA Las Vegas Vicinity Guide

From the junction of I-15 and US-95, take US-95 north to SR-157/Kyle Canyon and turn left, west. Drive about 20 miles on SR-157 to the junction with Echo Road at a sharp curve, about 0.5 miles past the Mt. Charleston fire station. Continue 0.4 miles to a FREE parking area on the right (restrooms). You can park here (for free) and walk the extra 0.1 mile on the pavement to the entrance of the Cathedral Rock Picnic Area. At press time, the fee to enter the picnic area was $6.00 for vehicles and $1.00 per walk-in (the other reason to park on the street and walk in). The South Loop trailhead is located just inside the Cathedral Rock Picnic Area across from the first parking area behind the entrance station.

Hiking

Map: USGS Charleston Peak (NV) 7.5-Minute (1:24,000 scale) Quad

This is a long, strenuous trip that needs to be started as early as possible—dawn preferably. The good thing, is that it is well-marked trail all the way. Dogs and their owners must be in excellent physical condition to hike Charleston from this route. The shortest way to do Charleston, but much steeper, is from the Lee Canyon Ski Area to the North Loop Trail. This knocks off about half the mileage.

Follow the South Loop-Charleston Peak Trail from the picnic area as it climbs up the canyon east of Echo Cliff, passing the broken debris of avalanches. In the summer, the aspens are in bloom, showing their pretty fluttering leaves amongst the pines. The trail ascends

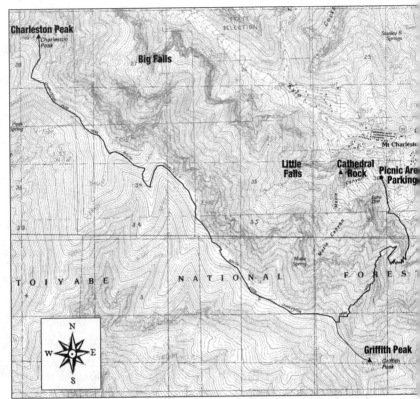

The South Loop Tail from Cathedral Picnic Area to Charleston Peak

steeply up to the main ridge. Just as you top off on the main ridge, Griffith Peak is off to your left. From this saddle at about 10,827' (3300 meters), the summit of Griffith is about 0.5 mile one-way. The trail to Charleston Peak continues to the right, northwesterly. Now that most of the gain is behind you, the hiking along the crest of the Spring Mountains, where the air is cool and the bristlecones pines grow profusely, is just wonderful. Just follow the trail to the summit, where views across the green pine-forested slopes out to the brown and pink desert below are spectacular.

Griffith Peak (11,072 ft; 3370.8 m) via South Loop Trail

Rating: Very strenuous
Recommended for: Well-conditioned dogs only!
Round-trip mileage: 9.2 miles, 3,650' gain, 8-9 hours
K9 water: No water; 2-quart minimum
Posted: Pets on leash. Clean up after your pet
Ambience: Tough workout to gain spectacular 360° views above timberline
Best time to hike: April to November

Driving

Maps: Nevada Road & Recreation Atlas, AAA Las Vegas Vicinity Guide

From the junction of I-15 and US-95, take US-95 north to SR-157 / Kyle Canyon and turn left, west. Drive about 20 miles on SR-157 to the junction with Echo Road at a sharp curve (about 0.5 miles past the

im and Duke on the way to Griffith Peak
from the South Loop Trail
PHOTO: Megan Lawlor

Mt. Charleston fire station). Continue 0.4 miles to a FREE parking area on the right (restrooms). You can park here (for free) and walk the extra 0.1 mile on the pavement to the entrance of the Cathedral Rock Picnic Area as the gate to the picnic area is sometimes locked. The signed South Loop trailhead is located just inside the Cathedral Rock Picnic Area across from the first parking area behind the entrance station.

Hiking

Map: USGS Griffith Peak (NV) 7.5-Minute (1:24,000 scale) Quad

Follow the South Loop-Charleston Peak Trail from the picnic area as it climbs up the canyon east of Echo Cliff, passing the broken debris of avalanches. The trail is very steep and tops out on the main ridge between Griffith and Charleston at about 10,827' (3300 meters). Head left, southeasterly, and scramble up Griffith Peak.

Harris Springs Road
Griffith Peak (11,072 ft; 3370.8 m)
From Harris Springs Road

Rating: Strenuous
Recommended for: Well-conditioned dogs only!
Round-trip mileage: 7.2 miles, 2,700' gain, 6-7 hours
K9 water: No water: 2-quart minimum
Recommended: Pets on leash. Clean up after your pet
Ambience: Shortest route to Griffith's summit
Best time to hike: April to November

Driving

Maps: Nevada Road & Recreation Atlas, AAA Las Vegas Vicinity Guide

From the junction of I-15 and US-95, take US-95 north to SR-157/Kyle Canyon and turn left, west. Drive about 12.6 miles to the dirt Harris Springs Road and turn left. Follow Harris Springs Road 2.3 miles to a fork. Go right at this fork and continue another 6.0 miles over rough road (high-clearance two-wheel drive vehicles should be OK) to the trailhead parking area.

Hiking

Maps: USGS Charleston Peak, Griffith Peak and La Madre Spring (NV) 7.5-Minute (1:24,000 scale) Quads

Follow the trail on the west side of the parking lot past the boulders. Walk the trail as it follows the old road about 2.1 miles to the rugged Griffith-Harris saddle (aka Kyle Canyon Overlook on the free USFS hiking trail pamphlet). Scramble and switchback up through a notch in the limestone cliffs, then up through open forests until a grassy slope is reached on Griffith's east ridge. Follow this ridge to the summit. This is the shortest route to Griffith Peak. It's about 1.5 miles from the saddle to the summit.

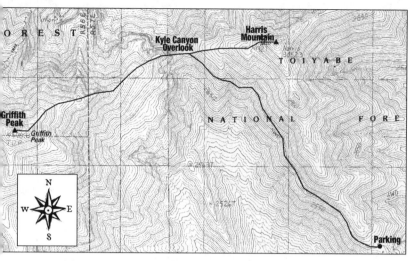

HARRIS MOUNTAIN (10.018 ft; 3052.3 m)
FROM HARRIS SPRINGS ROAD

Rating: Strenuous
Recommended for: Well-conditioned dogs only!
Round-trip mileage: 5.6 miles, 1,650' gain, 4-5 hours
K9 water: No water; 2-quart minimum
Recommended: Pets on leash. Clean up after your pet
Ambience: Nice walk along west ridge looking over at the La Madres
Best time to hike: April to November

Driving
Maps: Nevada Road & Recreation Atlas, AAA Las Vegas Vicinity Guide

From the junction of I-15 and US-95, take US-95 north to SR-157/Kyle Canyon and turn left, west. Drive about 12.6 miles to the dirt Harris Springs Road and turn left. Follow Harris Springs Road 2.3 miles to a fork. Go right at the fork and continue another 6.0 miles over rough road (high-clearance two-wheel drive should be OK) to the parking area and trailhead.

Hiking
Maps: USGS Charleston Peak, Griffith Peak and La Madre Spring (NV) 7.5-Minute (1:24,000 scale) Quads

From the parking lot hike past the boulder berm to the old Jeep trail.

Follow the old road about 2.1 miles along the west ridge of Harris Mountain to the saddle between Harris and Griffith Peak (on the left). Turn right, east and hike from the saddle about 0.7 miles up Harris Mountain's west ridge to it summit.

HARRIS MOUNTAIN AND GRIFFITH PEAK
Round-trip mileage: 8.6 miles, 3650' gain, 9-10 hours
In the mood for a really good workout?
Same driving and hiking instructions as for Griffith Peak from Harris Springs Road. Follow the trail on the west side of the parking lot, past the boulder berm. The trail essentially follows the Jeep trail all the way to the Griffith-Harris saddle. From the saddle scramble up Harris' west ridge. Zip back down to the saddle and hike over to Griffith Peak.

Justin Lawlor and Ginger at the old cabins at Deer Creek PHOTO: Megan Lawlor

DEER CREEK AND VICINITY

DEER CREEK

Rating: Easy
Recommended for: Small, out-of-shape or older dogs
Round-trip mileage: 1.0 miles, minimal gain, 1 hour
K9 water: Seasonal water; 1-quart minimum
Posted: Pets on leash. Clean up after your pet.
Ambience: A lovely spot for senior dogs with its year-round creek
Best time to hike: April to November

Driving

Maps: Nevada Road & Recreation Atlas, AAA Las Vegas Vicinity Guide

From the junction of I-15 and US-95, take US-95 north to SR-157/Kyle Canyon and turn left, west. Drive about 17.2 miles to SR-158 to Lee Canyon and turn right. Drive 5.5 miles to Deer Creek on your right

and park. Have your dog leashed before exiting the car since you have to cross the highway. After crossing, the trail starts behind the guard rail and heads south.

Hiking

Map: USGS Angel Peak (NV) 7.5-Minute (1:24,000 scale) Quad

There are about seven picnic tables spread along the creek, far enough apart to allow for privacy. The path is a paved road. Although this road is now blocked off there is parking across the street, just a short walk from the car. When we were children, our parents drove us on this road with picnic treats. It's now a short walk from the car and well worth the effort. For a more enjoyable trip, carry an ice chest

Wonderful family outings on Deer Creek PHOTO: Megan Lawlor

with wheels or have some friends help carry the food. Carry out all your trash and waste, as these areas are so vital to survival of wildlife. Deer Creek is great for the older dogs. The grade is easy, smooth and the walk about half an hour to the end of the picnic tables. Camping is allowed 100 yards from the creek and there are restrooms halfway up the path. It is a shady and cool retreat from the Las Vegas summer heat.

Notes

Deer Creek is probably one of the most reliable water sources in the Spring Mountains, supporting a variety of wildlife—mule deer, wild horses, Palmer chipmunks and many birds. The Palmer chipmunk with its white-striped back is found only on Mount Charleston, and nowhere else in the world!

In the late 1800s to early 1900s, the Deer Creek Sawmill was one of three main lumber operations supplying timber to Las Vegas and the construction of the Union Pacific Railway with lumber for its construction. In later years, timber came to Southern Nevada from neighboring states and the sawmill eventually closed. Some very old cabins in the upper regions of Deer Creek are remnants of the old mill days. Many of the cabins in the area are on private property. Not too long ago there were plans for a housing development. Those plans were abandoned. In 1966, in an exchange with property owners, the United States Forest Service acquired the land, preserving it for wildlife and future visitors to enjoy.

Robbers Roost Loop

Rating: Moderate
Recommended for: Well-conditioned dogs, any size
Round-trip mileage: 0.4 miles, 150', 30 minutes
K9 water: 1-quart minimum
Recommended: Pets on leash. Clean up after your pet.
Ambience: 1885 horse thief camp now a well-known bolted climbing route
Best time to hike: April to November

Driving

Maps: Nevada Road & Recreation Atlas, AAA Las Vegas Vicinity Guide

From the junction of I-15 and US-95, take US-95 north to SR-157/Kyle Canyon and turn left, west. Drive about 17.2 miles to SR-158 to Lee Canyon and turn right. Drive 3.4 miles to parking area on the right. The signed Robbers Roost trail is on the left side of the highway. Leash dogs for safety before getting out of the car on the highway.

Hiking

Map: USGS Angel Peak (NV) 7.5-Minute (1:24,000 scale) Quad

Walk across the highway to the trail. Walk a few feet up the trail and turn left. Follow the trail to a steep rock-hewn stairway. Head to the sandstone overhang and follow the trail under the overhang. It's short and steep and you'll have to catch your breath. Note the bolted rock routes up the overhanging rock—it looks like a tough climb! Continue on the path past the overhang to a grey box canyon and a small seasonal waterfall. Turn around to head back down the rocky trail and note a gentle flat trail off to the right. Take this long switch-back back down to the bottom of the original trail. It's a nice walk through the pines with a view across the canyon.

Hiking

This canyon was used by horse thieves in the mid-1800s to hide stolen horses, which were easily housed behind makeshift penstocks. Note the soot on the the rock walls from the old horse thief and rock climber campfires.

Inside the horse thieves lair at Robbers Roost PHOTO: Wynne Benti

North Loop to Rain Tree

Rating: Moderate
Recommended for: Well-conditioned dogs, any size
Round-trip mileage: 6.0 miles, 2,500' gain, 5-6 hours
K9 water: No water; 2-3 quart minimum
Posted: Pets on leash. Clean up after your pet.
Ambience: Shaded switchback trail to a magnificent bristlecone pine
Best time to hike: April to November

Driving
Maps: Nevada Road & Recreation Atlas, AAA Las Vegas Vicinity Guide
From the junction of I-15 and US-95, take US-95 north to SR-157/Kyle Canyon and turn left, west. Drive about 17.2 miles to SR-158 to Lee Canyon and turn right. Drive 4.8 miles to the parking area at the trail head on your left. On weekdays, there aren't too many people, but parking may be difficult on weekends. Parking is on your left.

Hiking
Maps: USGS Angel Peak and Charleston Peak (NV) 7.5-Minute (1:24,000 scale) Quads
Follow the shady trail from the parking area as it makes a gradual ascent. We hiked this trail in August and ran into lots of dogs. From Poodles to Rottweilers, most ranged from two to seven years old and were in good condition.

After hiking 1.5 miles, you'll come to a flat ridge with a small grove of bristlecone pines. From this ridge is a good view of Las Vegas. To the left of the city, looking east, is a white dome sitting atop Angel's Peak. It is a radar tracking station that was used during the 1960s by Nellis and McCarran airports to track planes.

After leaving this ridge, the trail continues with a series of switchbacks. The forest trees change as you gain elevation. You will pass over another ridge and here the gnarled and twisted trunks of the bristlecone pines weave themselves in and out of the path. Many of them look as if they are no longer alive, but they are.

At 2.7 miles, the trail levels into a large flat shaded area. The foot of Mummy Mountain looms above. This is the "Rain Tree," a beautiful, enormous bristlecone pine almost 3,000 years old. Its sheltering branches provide a great place for a picnic. Camping is discouraged

At the magnificent Rain Tree PHOTO: Megan Lawlor

due to the ecological sensitivity of the area.

For an added bonus, continue on to Mummy Springs via the marked trail to the right of the tree, which is about a half-mile further. The North Loop Trail, to the left of the tree, continues on to Charleston Peak.

The Big Meadow PHOTO: Wynne Benti

LEE CANYON AND VICINITY
BIG MEADOW AT OLD MILL

Rating: Super-easy
Recommended for: All dogs
Round-trip mileage: 0.5 miles, 150', 30 minutes
K9 water: 1-quart minimum
Recommended: Pets on leash. Clean up after your pet.
Ambience: Large roadside meadow with views of limestone cliffs
Best time to hike: April to November

Driving
Maps: Nevada Road & Recreation Atlas, AAA Las Vegas Vicinity Guide
From the junction of I-15 and US-95, take US-95 north to SR-156/Lee Canyon and turn left, west. Drive about 15 miles to Old Mill picnic area on the right. The meadow is just beyond the picnic area another 0.2 mile on the right. Park alongside the meadow just beyond Old Mill picnic area.

Hiking
Head west toward the peaks in the picture. Walk the circumference of the meadow for some exercise. Great for older dogs.

Lee Canyon Ski Area

Rating: Easy-moderate
Recommended for: Well-conditioned dogs, any size
Round-trip mileage: 1.5 miles, 750' gain, 1-2 hours
K9 water: Seasonal water in drainage above ski lift; 1-quart minimum
Recommended: Pets on leash. Clean up after your pet.
Ambience: Good workout up the ski slope, a little cross-country to cool water
Best time to hike: April to November

Driving

Maps: Nevada Road & Recreation Atlas, AAA Las Vegas Vicinity Guide

From the junction of I-15 and US-95, take US-95 north to SR-156/Lee Canyon and turn left, west. Drive about 17.3 miles to the ski area. Park in any of the parking spaces outside the ski area gate.

Hiking

Map: USGS Charleston Peak (NV) 7.5-Minute (1:24,000 scale) Quad

Pass through the gated entrance to the ski area, and walk down the road to the main lodge in the center of the ski area (a row of portable restrooms is located on its back flank). From the center ski lodge building follow the middle ski lift (most westerly and currently painted black) up the grassy hill to its end, staying left. Turn left on a dirt road just past the end of the lift. Follow the dirt road a short way to a narrow canyon filled with avalanche debris from the heavy winter of 2005. Pick your way straight across the canyon to our destination, a narrow boulder-filled creek that drains the high ridges of the Spring Mountains. There is water here all summer, and the forested area to the west of the gully is blanketed with wildflowers in early summer. To the right of this gully is the ridge up to the North Loop Trail, the fastest way to Charleston Peak (next page). Nice views above Lee Canyon and cool water make for a lovely picnic spot.

CHARLESTON PEAK (11,915 ft; 3631.7 m)
VIA LEE CANYON SKI AREA

Rating: Very strenuous, cross-country and trail, Class 2 with route finding
Recommended for: Well-conditioned dogs only!!
Round-trip mileage: 10.0 miles, 3,400' gain, 8 hours
K9 water: Seasonal water above ski lift, none on the trail; 3-quart minimum
Posted: Pets on leash. Clean up after your pet.
Ambience: Up a super steep, gnarly ridge and on to the trail just 3.5 miles below Charleston's Summit!
Best time to hike: April to November

Driving

Maps: Nevada Road & Recreation Atlas, AAA Las Vegas Vicinity Guide

From the junction of I-15 and US-95, take US-95 north to SR-156/Lee Canyon and turn left, west. Drive about 17.3 miles to the ski area. Park in any of the parking spaces outside the ski area gate.

Hiking

Map: USGS Charleston Peak (NV) 7.5-Minute (1:24,000 scale) Quad

Walk down to the main lodge in the center of the ski area (a row of portable restrooms are located on its back flank). From the ski lodge follow the middle (most westerly) ski lift up to its end, staying left. Turn left on a dirt road and cross over an avalanche debris basin to a boulder-filled creek in a narrow limestone gully. This in itself is a lovely place to have a picnic (see previous trail description).

From here pick your way up the stream but get on the right, west side of the stream on a very steep forested ridge of loose dirt, trees, with some Class 2 scrambling over limestone ledges. As your near the top and see blue sky, stay to the right side of the narrowing ridge. You are shooting for elevation 3441-meters, as shown on the USGS Charleston Peak Quad (1994), which will bring you out right on the Charleston Peak Trail.

After all this rugged, steep slogging, holding on to tree trunks and limbs to pull yourself up, you pop out right on the trail. And there, to the right, west, isCharleston Peak, only 3.5 miles away! As you stand on the trail at this spot, make a mental note of your physical landmarks for the return route so you don't inadvertently miss it and end up on Echo Drive in Kyle Canyon!

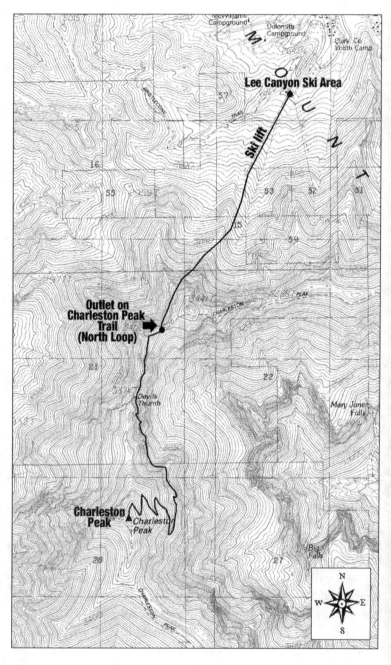

Bristlecone Loop Trail
via Lee Canyon Ski Area

Rating: Easy-moderate
Recommended for: Well-conditioned dogs, any size
Round-trip mileage: 5.5 miles, 1,300 gain, 3.5-4 hours
K9 water: 2-3-quart minimum
Posted: Pets on leash. Clean up after your pet.
Ambience: Easy to follow trail with beautiful scenery
Best time to hike: April to November

Driving

Maps: Nevada Road & Recreation Atlas, AAA Las Vegas Vicinity Guide

From the junction of I-15 and US-95, take US-95 north to SR-156/Lee Canyon and make a left. Drive 17.3 miles until you reach the ski area. The road dead ends in the upper parking lot just around the corner from the ski area entrance. The trailhead for upper Bristlecone Loop starts on the west side of the parking area.

Hiking

Map: USGS Charleston Peak (NV) 7.5-Minute (1:24,000 scale) Quad

This trail is one of very few trails in the Lee Canyon area, most often visited in the winter for its wonderful ski area. Although its skiing may not compare to Tahoe or Aspen, it's only an hour's drive from Las Vegas and packed with fun. The ski area has been around for over forty years. Even earlier in 1941, when the U.S. Forest service began looking at the Lee Canyon area for it's winter sports potential, skiers were towed by ropes behind horse drawn sleds on the site of the present day ski slopes. There are presently thirteen runs with three ski lifts and enough challenging runs to satisfy the expert and beginner. Lee Canyon also offers a nice snack bar and cozy bar/lounge with warm fireplace.

The beginning of the upper Bristlecone Loop Trail starts just above the ski area parking lot and in the summer it may be possible to see wild horses grazing on the grassy ski slopes. The upper portion of the trail starts as a narrow, easy to follow trail with plenty of shade. It winds through gorgeous groves of aspen and white fir trees and switchbacks along until you reach the bristlecone pine trees, just

Practicing for longer overnight trips PHOTO: Megan Lawlor

below timberline. The bristlecones grow in only six western states at altitudes of 8,000 to 11,000 feet. They survive extremely harsh conditions and live to be thousands of years old. Perhaps the hardiest tree in the world, the needles stay on their limbs for over 40 years!

The top here is lovely with nice views of the surrounding mountains. As the first half of the trail begins to level off and start a gradual downhill, the trail becomes a wide gravel abandoned road. The lower portion doesn't offer as much shade, but it's an easy walk with places just off the trail to sit and let your dog cool off. If you decide to do the entire loop the lower portion of Bristlecone loop lets you out onto SR-156 where you have to walk up the paved road back to the upper parking lot. Be sure to have your dog leashed and watch for vehicles.

COLD CREEK
ALONG THE ROAD TO WHEELER PASS

From the confines of a deep cave, the small band of Native Americans watched silently as rain drizzled in the valley and lightning careened across the black canopy of sky, igniting flames of red that erupted on the mountainside, growing with each puff of wind until at last it enveloped the highest peak. For untold days and nights, the land resembled Gehenna, cooking and charring every living thing in its path until one night the sky opened up. Torrents of rain flooded the mountain. Sheets of water rushed into the canyons until the last glow of red was obliterated.

The holocaust blackened the land as far as the eye could see. Trees, once heavy with cones and foliage, were stripped of their bark and stood in grotesque positions. Inside the sanctuary of the cave, the Paiutes thanked the "Great Spirit" for sparing their lives. Nature's forces turned this section of the Toiyabe Forest into a mountain of spector-silvery wood ghosts that march silently up the hillsides.

From verdant sylvan glades in lower Wheeler Canyon to the desolate, the change is startling. Stark white trees, their branches twisted and scarred, to the towering pinons that remained untouched those many years ago. And this is where we love to walk our dogs. They love the climbs to the steep hillsides and refresh themselves in the water that courses from a clear spring to form a creek that winds through a jungle of willows, squaw bush, cress, rushes. Giant alamos (cottonwoods) and pinyon spread a blanket of shade over the entire area, while miniature waterfalls cascade over moss-covered rocks.

The hikes in the Cold Creek area are perfect for all our furry friends, whether they are in extreme good health, somewhat older or just a little portly. Remember to keep them on a leash, lest they chase

Wild horse watering hole about a half-mile off the old Wheeler Pass Road
PHOTO: Wynne Benti

the wildlife.

Most high-clearance two-wheel drives should make it to the Willow Springs area. About a mile after Willow Springs, the road to Wheeler Pass is NOT recommended for stock four-wheel drive vehicles. It is rock strewn, loose and steep. However it makes a nice seven mile round-trip, waterless hike along the road from the second pull-out at Willow Springs.

WILD HORSE WATERING HOLES
(UNOFFICIAL NAME)

Rating: Easy
Recommended for: All dogs
Round-trip mileage: 1.0 mile, minimal gain, 30 minutes
K9 water: Water year-round
Recommended: Dogs on leash
Ambience: High desert ponds created to water the wild horse herd
Best time to hike: Year-round with early morning starts in summer

Driving
Maps: Nevada Road & Recreation Atlas, AAA Las Vegas Vicinity Guide

From the junction of I-15 and US-95, take US-95 north to Cold Creek (there are two prisons at this intersection) and turn left, west, and follow the paved road 12.7 miles to signed USFS 601 (good dirt), just after the fire station, a large steel building, on the right side of the Cold Creek road. Turn immediate left into a pullout and park next to a picnic table, USFS information kiosk, and an old ruin.

Hiking
Map: USGS Cold Creek (NV) 7.5-Minute (1:24,000 scale) Quad

Walk across the dirt road, USFS 601 to signed USFS 587, the dirt road that runs east behind the fire station. Walk the road pass a pond on the left, then one on the right. Continue a half mile to the road end in a large luxurious pond, somewhat chalky from the high mineral content in the water. With great views, summer evenings are wonderful at this spot watching the Sheep Mountains cast their long dark shadows across the vast, waterless alluvial plain below.

Hiking

For some reason, the two state prisons situated at the edge of US-95 and Cold Creek are a deterrent to many visitors, so most of the time you'll have this place to yourself.

Trail of the Mustangs
(Unofficial Name)

Rating: Easy, cross-country
Recommended for: All dogs
Round-trip mileage: 1.25miles, 60' gain, 40 minutes
K9 water: WATER year-round
Recommended: Dogs on leash
Ambience: Beautiful little creek through high desert scrub and junipers
Best time to hike: Year-round with early morning starts in summer

Driving

Maps: Nevada Road & Recreation Atlas, AAA Las Vegas Vicinity Guide

From the junction of I-15 and US-95, take US-95 north to Cold Creek and turn left, west, and follow the paved road 12.7 miles to dirt USFS 601. At this intersection is a picnic table, creek and an old ruin, a wonderful place to stop. Turn right on signed USFS 601 (good dirt). At 0.5 miles stay right at a fork. At 0.7 miles, where the dirt road crosses a creek, park at a loop on the left side of the dirt road.

Hiking

Map: USGS Cold Creek (NV) 7.5-Minute (1:24,000 scale) Quad

Along Cold Creek PHOTO: Wynne Benti

From the parking area follow the path along the creek, well-worn by the herd of wild mustangs that live in this area. Their path follows this pleasant creek up a gently sloping canyon, meandering from side to side, through stands of scrub live oak and a multitude of wildflowers during late spring and early summer.

The path eventually peters out near the top of the canyon, just below private property, delineated by a chain link fence spanning the canyon.

Rosy wanders along Willow Creek to the old Wheeler Pass Road   PHOTO: Wynne Benti

Willow Creek

Rating: Super-easy
Recommended for: All dogs
Round-trip mileage: Varies
K9 water: WATER year-round
Recommended: Dogs on leash
Ambience: Natural riparian habitat—carry out all trash
Best time to visit: April to November

Driving
Maps: Nevada Road & Recreation Atlas, AAA Las Vegas Vicinity Guide
From the junction of I-15 and US-95, take US-95 north to Cold Creek and turn left, west. Follow the paved road 12.7 miles to its intersection with USFS 601. At this intersection is a picnic table, creek and an old ruin, a wonderful place to stop. Turn right, north, on a good dirt road, USFS 601 and drive 3.1 miles to Willow Creek and a pullout on the right. Park here.

Hiking
Maps: USGS Cold Creek and Willow Creek (NV) 7.5-Minute (1:24,000 scale) Quads
There is an interpretive sign here noting that the creek is being restored to its natural habitat following years of damage by motorized vehicles driving along the stream bank. From the parking area follow the path along the creek, well-worn by the herd of wild mustangs that live in this area. There is a pedestrian bypass into the riparian area behind the sign, but no specific trail. We like to walk along the road to the next pullout just little over a quarter-mile up the road.

This is the old Jeep road to Wheeler Pass. About a mile past the pullout mentioned above, the road gets incredibly rough and will cause damage to your vehicle. It was not always in such poor condition and was once passable all the way to Pahrump in a two-wheel drive vehicle, but that was a very long time ago.

Notes
Willow Creek is a very popular on summer weekends. The old road to Wheeler Pass is a well-known ATV route, so expect possible off-road noise and activity on weekends.

Bonanza Peak

Rating: Strenuous
Recommended for: Well-conditioned dogs only!!
Round-trip mileage: 9 miles, 2,900' gain, 6-8 hours
K9 water: No water; 2-3 quart minimum
Posted: Pets on leash. Clean up after your pet
Ambience: Remote shaded trail shaded to great desert vistas of Pahrump Valley and Cold Creek
Best time to hike: April to November

Driving

Maps: Nevada Road & Recreation Atlas, AAA Las Vegas Vicinity Guide

From the junction of I-15 and US-95, take US-95 north to Cold Creek and turn left, west. Drive about 12.7 miles to the intersection of USFS 601, the road to Wheeler Pass. Stay left on the paved road and continue 3.1 miles to the Bonanza trailhead. Just past the community of Cold Creek the road becomes dirt and there are no facilities in Cold Creek, the closest being in Indian Springs. All vehicles should be able to reach the trailhead. The trail begins to the left of the sign.

Hiking

Maps: USGS Charleston Peak and Cold Creek (NV) 7.5-Minute (1:24,000 scale) Quads

Bonanza Peak has to be one of our all-time favorite hikes because of its remoteness and opportunity to view wild horses. We have seen beautifully marked paints that stood out starkly against the landscape. The habitat for these non-native species is dwindling so keep your distance and your dog under control so they can feed and drink without being disturbed.

The beginning of the trail takes you through a small, grassy meadow and climbs at a gradual ascent. Although this hike reaches high elevations, it is a trail that requires no technical skill but plenty of endurance. The heavily wooded trail provides plenty of shade. There have been a few fires here that have burned thousands of acres. It takes generations for the forest to recover. Miniature forests of scrub oak seem to have replaced the pines in the lower regions.

After maneuvering many switchbacks (maybe 100) you'll reach the ridge where the scenery is absolutely breathtaking. To the west,

View from Bonanza Peak PHOTO: Megan Lawlor

Pahrump Valley, the mountains of Death Valley; to the east the Sheep Mountains and Desert National Wildlife Range. The wind often whips across this ridge so watch your footing. The trail continues south, ascending a few steep, rocky areas then comes out on the west side of the mountain. Here, it levels somewhat, ascending more gradually through the quiet forest.

Traverse several switchbacks that head to the summit, but not directly. We passed the summit the first time we did the peak as there was no obvious place to leave the trail.

To find the cutoff point to the summit, look for a rocky outcropping of limestone cliffs on the left. If you start heading downhill on switchbacks, you have gone too far. Head back toward the limestone cliffs in the wooded saddle (sometimes there is a cairn just off the trail) and pass the limestone diagonally in a southeast direction. Follow the ridge line south about a quarter-mile and two hundred feet to the summit.

The summit register is marked with a cairn. The summit is a bit precarious in some places so watch your footing. The views of Charleston Peak from here are really nice, also. Return by the same route.

Mountain Springs Summit
and Vicinity

Potosi Mine

Rating: Easy
Recommended for: Well-conditioned dogs, any size
Round-trip mileage: 1.0 miles, 525' gain, 1-2 hours to poke around
K9 water: No water; 2-quart minimum
Recommended: Dogs on leash–mine shafts in area
Ambience: Oldest mine in Nevada
Best time to hike: October to March

Driving

Maps: Nevada Road & Recreation Atlas, AAA Las Vegas Vicinity Guide

From the junction of I-15 and US-95, take I-15 south towards Los Angeles, to SR-160/Blue Diamond Rd. exit. Drive west on SR-160

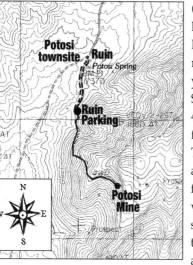

(towards Pahrump) approximately 18.5 miles to the signed Potosi Mountain dirt road (the sign is missing at times) and turn left (if you hit Mountain Springs Summit, you've gone to far). Drive 4.3 miles to Potosi Spring (an A-frame building is on the right). Two wheel-drives should park along the main road and hike in from here. Four-wheel drives can veer left, then straight across the spring on the road about 0.3 miles to the lower mine mill, and park, at about elevation 5741'.

Hiking

Map: USGS Potosi (NV) 7.5-Minute (1:24,000 scale) Quad

The main mining area is not visible from the parking area. From the parking area at the mill ruins, follow the trail on the south side of the ruins across a narrow wash (and an illegible sign). The trail begins to climb up and around the mountain side. Follow the route carefully as

Skull rock on the Potosi mine trail
PHOTO: Wynne Benti

it is easy to miss the trail. Some painted yellow arrows are helpful. The trail finally reaches a viewpoint and the mine with its large tailings piles is before you. Walk along the trail to the tailings piles. Not much remains, just a few remnants of the large structures used to haul the giant ore buckets up and down the slope. In winter there may be snow. The summit of Mt. Potosi is over 8,000 feet in elevation.

The old Potosi Mine is one of our favorite destinations. We love to walk our dogs any time and any where, but it's really special to be able to bring them along to Potosi, where we relive some state history as well as getting our exercise. In Spanish, the word "Potosi" means rich or great wealth. The Paiutes were the first to discover that the mountain contained a lot of heavy rock.

Mormon settlers were next to investigate the ore, which assayed out so favorably that in June of 1855, N. V. Jones dispatched 15 men to begin the operation of Potosi Mine. Ore smelting required water, so a large furnace was erected near a spring at the base of the mountain, the first smelter ever built or operated in Nevada. The ore proved disappointing. It's bullets clogged rifles, while its overall content was shiny and brittle instead of dull and soft, as lead should be. Trouble with the local Paiutes, dwindling sales and a vanishing water supply, forced Jones to close the mine, making Potosi Nevada's first ghost town.

In the midst of all the trouble at Potosi, an alert group of miners analyzed the content of the ore and found it contained far more silver

Above: Tailings piles high on the Potosi mine trail Below: Inside the mine PHOTOS: Wynne Benti

than lead. In 1860, they formed the Colorado Mining Company and resumed operations. The ore proved irritatingly complex, difficult to melt and even more difficult to separate. It contained a high content of zinc, as well as sulphur that burned easily.

A new hundred-ton reduction mill in the nearby town of Goodsprings made Potosi the major zinc producer in the territory. In 1913, Potosi was a key supplier of zinc during World War I and by 1926, had produced over 30,000 tons of ore. But again, operations did not prove economically sound and Potosi gasped her last breath.

Today, a trip to Potosi provides a brief glimpse to our past mining heritage. Juniper trees lend a refreshing touch of greenery to the area. High on the eastern skyline in the layers of gray limestone, is a row of window rock carved by wind. The limestone contains fabulous specimens of ancient fossils. A huge boulder weighing several tons is perched upon a two-foot square pedestal.

Potosi Mountain (8514')

Rating: Difficult-strenuous! Cross-country requiring good route-finding and map reading skills
Recommended for: Well-conditioned dogs, medium-sized and above
Round-trip mileage: 9 miles, 2,700' gain, 6-7 hours
K9 water: No water; 3-quart minimum
Ambience: Ferns, coral and ammonites imbedded in limestone on a hike that looks more rugged than it is. Beautiful hike for a crisp winter's day.
Best time to hike: November to March

Driving

Maps: Nevada Road & Recreation Atlas, AAA Las Vegas Vicinity Guide

From the junction of I-15 and US-95, take I-15 south towards Los Angeles, to SR-160/Blue Diamond Rd. exit. Drive west on SR-160 (towards Pahrump) approximately 18.5 miles to the signed Potosi Mountain dirt road (the sign is missing at times) and turn left (if you hit Mountain Springs Summit, you've gone to far). The Potosi Mountain road is recommended for four-wheel drives as it is washed out in places.

Set your odometer to zero. Drive 4.3 miles to Potosi Spring (on the left), and stay right on the main road. At 5.2 miles go left at the signed fork "Goodsprings 17, Sandy 10, Rough Road Ahead" (this sign has been missing in the past so make sure to watch your mileage). At 6.4 miles reach a short steep hill with some loose large rocks. Just past the hill, fork left. Drive another 0.25 miles and fork left again. Drive an additional 1.4 miles NE to a cabin on the left and park (about 8.0 miles from Blue Diamond Road).

Hiking

Map: USGS Potosi (NV) 7.5-Minute (1:24,000 scale) Quad

Hike up the wash to the right of the cabin to high-walled chasm where the wash narrows and an impressive (usually dry) waterfall which is bypassed on the left. Embedded in the grey limestone of the waterfall are the perfectly defined patterns of broad coral leaves, more than 300 million years old–deposited when the area was covered by warm seas. Shells and other fossils are visible in the rock in the wash and all the way up the ridge to the summit of Potosi. Follow

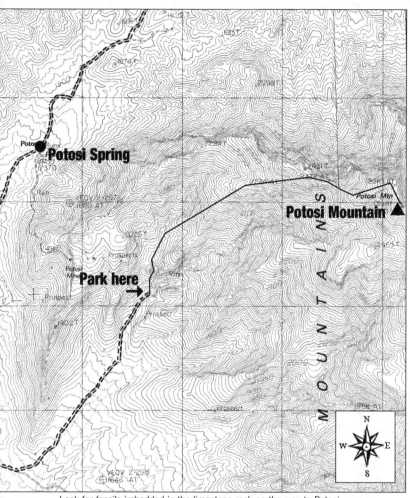

Look for fossils imbedded in the limestone rock on the way to Potosi

the ridge between forks to 2,234'. Continue on to 2,431' to a saddle and continue about 0.5 miles more to the summit.

This is an interesting and wonderful way to the summit of Potosi. The north-facing slopes can be completely covered in snow with only a few patches near the summit. From the summit, you can see from San Gorgonio to the Pine Valley Mountains in Utah—Telescope, Sentinel, Porter and the crest of the Sierra to the west.

CARPENTER CANYON
OUT OF PAHRUMP

Rating: Hiking is easy
Driving: Rugged 4x4 only, 12.5 miles on rugged four-wheel drive road
Recommended for: All dogs
Round-trip hiking: 0.3 miles
K9 water: Water; 1-quart minimum
Ambience: Beautiful location high in the pines along a year-round creek
Best time to hike: Year-round. October to April. Hot in summer on approach road. Snow and possible heavy runoff in winter.

Driving

Maps: Nevada Road & Recreation Atlas, AAA Las Vegas Vicinity Guide
One-way driving mileage: 12.5 miles of rugged road

From the junction of I-15 and US-95, take I-15 south towards Los Angeles, to SR-160/Blue Diamond Rd. exit. Drive west on SR-160 (towards Pahrump) approximately 45.7 miles to the signed Carpenter Canyon 4x4 dirt road and set your odometer to zero. At 1.0 mile, pass the fire station. The road heads up the broad alluvial fan and open desert. If you love the open desert the view is beautiful, it is difficult to imagine any greenery or water anywhere in this area. Despite its hardy approach across the exposed desert alluvial fan, people travel this road all year to get up to the cool shaded canyon.

At 9.4 miles, the road drops down deeply into the canyon. The top of this drop is as far as the high-clearance two-wheel drive vehicles should go. Only four-wheel drive should continue down into the canyon. From this point is about three miles to the end of the road which meanders from here through a pebbly wash. At about 11.7 miles, you'll reach water, then make several stream crossings before entering the forest of high pines and the end of the road at 12.5 miles.

Walking

At the end of the road is a USFS information kiosk with a map of the area. There are no trails out of Carpenter Canyon, just the old jeep trail to the right and across the creek from the kiosk. Cross the creek and follow the old track along the creek to a high-walled narrows. A large tree, stripped of all its bark, has fallen across the narrows. It is a

Jeff and Rosy along the creek in Carpenter Canyon   PHOTO: Wynne Benti

beautiful yet curious sight, almost as if someone placed it there.

Notes

Florine Lawlor first explored Carpenter Canyon with her grandfather in 1935 back when Hwy. 160 didn't exist. The quickest way from Las Vegas to Pahrump was over the old bladed gravel road to Pahrump (Potato Pass) now known as the Rocky Gap 4x4 Road from Willow Springs in Red Rock. The Manse Ranch with its fresh fruit and vegetables was all there was in Pahrump.

CONTACT MINE LOOP
GOODSPRINGS MINING DISTRICT

Rating: Moderate
Recommended for: Well-conditioned dogs, any size
Round-trip mileage: 4.0 miles, 200' gain, 2 hours to poke around
K9 water: No water; 2-quart minimum
Recommended: Dogs on leash–mine shafts in area. Leash-free area
Ambience: One of the oldest mines and rock quarry areas in Southern Nevada
Best time to hike: November to March. Get an early morning start.

Driving
Maps: Nevada Road & Recreation Atlas, AAA Las Vegas Vicinity Guide

From the junction of I-15 and US-95, take I-15 south towards Los Angeles, to SR 161/Exit 12-Jean/Goodsprings. Exit and at the end of the off-ramp turn right, north to Goodsprings. At 5.4 miles turn right on the paved Goodsprings Bypass Gravel Haul Route. There is an active quarry along this road, so watch for big haul trucks during the week. Set your odometer to zero and follow the paved road 1.9 miles to a stop sign, turn right (town of Goodsprings is left).

Old jar PHOTO: Wynne Benti

Continue on the paved road. In the distance, you'll see a prominent road climbing up the south end of Potosi Mountain. This road was open to the public many years ago. It was permanently closed because of all the radio towers on the mountain, and the fact that it was so steep that Clark County tired of the liability associated with the vehicles that have bee wrecked or stuck on it. Just below the first set of towers, now operated by the FAA, was the site of the plane crash that claimed actress Carole Lombard's life. You'll see a lot of planes coming into McCarren at this spot. At 3.2, fork, stay left. At 6.3 miles stay left at the fork (Las Vegas Rock Rainbow Quarries is on the right). The road turns to dirt. At 6.9, turn right onto spur dirt road. This is USFS 507 and it is washed out! Park here. Do not attempt to drive the road.

View of the McCullough Mountains from the old quarry PHOTO: Wynne Benti

Hiking

Map: USGS Cottonwood Pass (NV) 7.5-Minute (1:24,000 scale) Quad

This is a lovely hikes especially on an overcast winter's day. sadly, there was a huge fire in here just a few years ago, so the landscape was burned. The fire actually uncovered many intact glass bottles that were hidden for years in the desert scrub.

From the car, walk straight ahead a short distance and turn right at a barrier of red sandstone boulders, climb a short incline and turn left following a red sand road that parallels the pink hills on the right. The walking on this upper road is much easier than on the rocky, washed out USFS 507 just below. Up the road a short way pass a USFS 507 road sign. Stay on the road as it follows along the pink hills. This was an active mine and quarry for many years and the miners

The Contact Mine PHOTO: Wynne Benti

old camping spots can still be found along this route, lots of old cans and broken glass. Unfortunately, the fire really did a lot of damage. About a half hour into the hike note large rock cairns, old mining claim markers on either side of the road.

About forty minutes into the hike, turn right on a road that goes up on to the pink hills and into the old quarry area. As this road tops out, continue following it as it turns left, east. The views from up here are just beautiful. Looking northwest across the pink hills on the east slope of Potosi Mountain, a large tailings pile comes into view, those of the Contact Mine. Follow the quarry road down off the hill to the main road and head to the mines. Leash your dogs around the mines, though most of the shafts have been filled in or covered by chain link. The trail north up over the hill goes to the old Pauline Mine. Complete the loop back cars by following the main dirt road back.

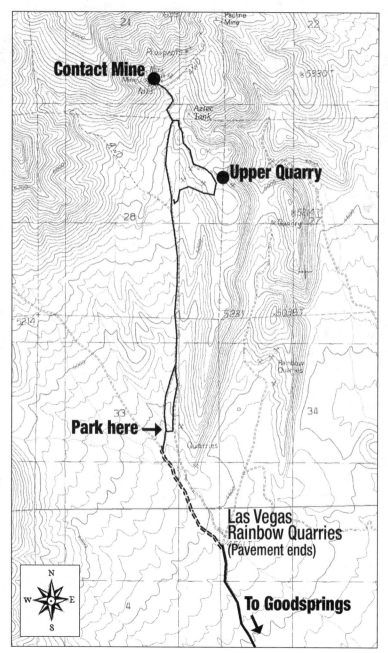

Contact Mine

Upper Quarry

Park here →

Las Vegas
Rainbow Quarries
(Pavement ends)

To Goodsprings

Table Mountain
Goodsprings Mining District

Rating: Moderate
Recommended for: Well-conditioned dogs, any size
Round-trip mileage: 2.5 miles, 600' gain, 1.5 hours
K9 water: No water; 2-quart minimum
Recommended: Dogs on leash–mine shafts in area. Leash-free area.
Ambience: Beautiful flat mesa in the heart of the Mojave above Goodsprings
Best time to hike: November to March. Get an early morning start.

Driving

Maps: Nevada Road & Recreation Atlas, AAA Las Vegas Vicinity Guide

From the junction of I-15 and US-95, take I-15 south towards Los Angeles, to SR 161/Exit 12-Jean/Goodsprings. Exit and at the end of the off-ramp turn right, north to Goodsprings. Drive 6.2 miles to a fork. Stay left at the fork and drive 3.5 miles to Columbia Pass (4,400'). The road is paved and passable to all cars. Carefully turn around at Columbia Pass and drive east to a dirt road on the right, just east of the pass. A two-wheel drive with good clearance can drive about a mile up the road to an obvious fork at the Argentina Mine Workings. Park here and get some exercise!

Hiking

Map: USGS Goodsprings (NV) 7.5-Minute (1:24,000 scale) Quad

Walk up the right fork of the road to the summit plateau, then west to the Table benchmark. This beautiful mesa is volcanic in origin.

THE SHEEP RANGE
DESERT NATIONAL WILDLIFE REFUGE

The Desert National Wildlife Range, which shares its northern perimeter with Nellis Air Force Base, was established in 1936 as a habitat for bighorn sheep. It encompasses over 1.5 million acres and six major mountain ranges, making it the largest National Wildlife Refuge in the lower forty-eight.

All of the hikes listed in this section are accessible, but conditions are constantly changing. As of press time, it was not possible to complete the Alamo Road from DNWR to Pahranagat NWR as it was closed past Cabin Springs due to hazardous road conditions near the dry lake bed. Apparently a few vehicles were stranded necessitating rescues (there was no cell phone reception). Current conditions for the Alamo Road can be found at <http://desertcomplex.fws.gov>. Check ahead before planning a round-trip venture on the Alamo Road, on the previously mentioned website or by calling Pahranagat NWR or DNWR headquarters. Their phone numbers listed in the back of the book under *Important Contact Numbers*.

THE SHEEP MOUNTAINS
DESERT NATIONAL WILDLIFE REFUGE

The Desert National Wildlife Range encompasses over 1.5 million acres of diverse desert shrub and coniferous forest habitat for the desert bighorn sheep and many other species.

To Pahranagat Wildlife Refuge
(check for road closures)

EAST DESERT RANGE

SAWMILL SPRING

HAYFORD PEAK

Wire Grass Spring (cabin site)

HIDDEN FOREST

SHEEP RANGE

Alamo Road (The Old Road to Alamo)

COW CAMP

JOE MAY CANYON

MORMON WELL

Historic Mormon Well was first recorded in 1896 and has since served as a watering hole for travelers and livestock. The old corral on the north side is listed in the National Register of Historical Places.

Mormon Well Road

Carrying, possessing or discharging firearms, or other explosives including fireworks, inside the refuge is strictly prohibited.

LAS VEGAS RANGE

Agave Roasting Pit

Sheep Mountain Range Bighorn Habitat

CORN CREEK FIELD STATION

US 95

TO LAS VEGAS

N
W   E
S

©2005 SDP INC. Map not to scale

Corn Creek Field Station
INTERPRETIVE WALK

Rating: Super easy
Recommended for: Small, out-of-shape or older dogs
Mileage: 0.75 miles round-trip, minimal gain, 40 minutes
K9 water: Water; 1-quart minimum
Ambience: Lush shaded oasis and picnic area in the middle of the desert
Best time to walk: Year-round

Driving
Maps: Nevada Road & Recreation Atlas, AAA Las Vegas Vicinity Guide
From the junction of I-15 and US-95, take US-95 north to Corn Creek Road and turn right, east. Drive approximately 4.0 miles to the Visitor Center.

Hiking
Map: USGS Corn Creek Springs (NV) 7.5-Minute (1:24,000 scale) Quad
The signed trail starts to the left of the interpretive kiosk. This area was inhabited up to 12,000 years ago by the nomadic ancestors of the Southern Paiutes. Wagon trains started stopping here on their way

The old homestead PHOTO: Wynne Benti

west, and later a store house for the railroad was built here to store railroad ties and supplies. The Richardsons, a Mormon family from Utah settled here in 1916 and planted the fruit orchards and nut trees. Their cabin, chicken coop and some of the old orchard trees are still here. When Corn Creek was included in the designation of the Desert National Wildlife Refuge, it was made the refuge headquarters.

Just pass the old cabin is a remarkable sight, an aquarium housed within a small building with windows that look on to the underwater habitat of the Pahrump poolfish. One spring in Pahrump was the only home to this endangered species. Before the spring completely dried up in 1975, twenty-nine of these tiny fish were moved to a pond here, and eventually this aquarium and to two other locations in Nevada to ensure their survival. Had they not been moved the Pahrump poolfish would have become extinct, gone forever.

Agave roasting pit high in Joe May PHOTO: Wynne Benti

JOE MAY CANYON
AGAVE ROASTING PIT

Rating: Moderate-strenuous
Recommended for: Well-conditioned dogs, medium-sized and above
Mileage: 4 miles round-trip, ' gain, 2-3 hours
K9 water: Water; 2-3 quart minimum
Best time to hike: November to April

Driving
Map: Nevada Road & Recreation Atlas, AAA Las Vegas Vicinity Guide
From the junction of I-15 and US-95, take US-95 north to Corn Creek Road and turn right, east. Drive approximately 4.0 miles to the Visitor Center. Just past the Visitor Center, turn left on the Alamo Road and set your odometer to zero. Drive 3.0 miles to Joe May Canyon and turn right. Continue up the rugged road (high clearance two-wheel drives should make it) At 7.1 miles pass a pen stock. Two-wheel drives should park here. Four-wheel drives continue to the end of the road at 7.5 miles, marked by the BLM Wilderness Boundary sign. Do not continue driving into the wash as tempting as it may be!

Hiking
Map: USGS Black Hills (NV) 7.5-Minute (1:24,000 scale) Quad
Follow the old Jeep track past the wilderness marker as it drops a few feet down into the wash that enters the main canyon. The track weaves in and out the center of the canyon, and soon vanishes, beneath a myriad of streambed channels, rocks and boulders. Pick any route that is easy walking. Now and then you'll see an errant duck placed by someone. Look for impressions of ancient coral in the rocks from old Cambrian era seas that covered the area almost 540 million years ago.

The canyon eventually narrows and large pinyons compliment desert cactus, agave and yucca. Just before some dark limestone pinnacles look for a fabulous specimen of an agave roasting pit. Trail continues up the canyon and deadends at a foundation once used for a water tank at the base of Wildhorse Pass.

Old cabin at Wiregrass Spring PHOTO: Wynne Benti

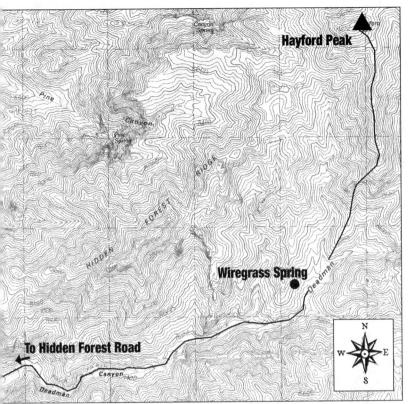

DEADMAN CANYON TO WIREGRASS SPRING AND THE HIDDEN FOREST

Rating: Moderate-strenuous
Recommended for: Well-conditioned dogs, any size
Mileage: 10 miles round-trip, 2100' gain, 6-7 hours
K9 water: Water; 2-3 quart minimum
Best time to hike: November to April. Get an early morning start.

Driving

Maps: Nevada Road & Recreation Atlas, AAA Las Vegas Vicinity Guide

From the junction of I-15 and US-95, take US-95 north to Corn Creek Road and turn right, east. Drive approximately 4.0 miles to the Visitor Center. Just past the Visitor Center, turn left on the Alamo Road and set your odometer to zero. Drive approximately 16.0 miles to Hidden Forest Road and turn right, east. At 19.6 reach the end of the road at a locked gate. This is Deadman Canyon, elevation 5,810'. Park here, careful not to block the gate.

540 million year old fossilized coral
PHOTO: Wynne Benti

Hiking

Map: USGS Black Hills, Hayford Peak and Sheep Peak (NV) 7.5-Minute (1:24,000 scale) Quad

This trail can be done as dayhike or an overnight backpack with a camp at Wiregrass Spring. From the seemingly bleak and shadeless parking area, it is difficult to imagine that there is any kind of forest hidden within this vast expanse of limestone ridges and canyons. From the gate follow the road up Deadman Canyon, from arid desert and Joshua trees, through pinyon and juniper, to Ponderosa, spruce, white fir and aspen—truly remarkable. Just follow the road, then the trail up the canyon until you reach Wiregrass Spring and an old cabin. Over the years this cabin has been lovingly

Cabin at Wiregrass
WATERCOLOR: Wynne Benti

maintained by the hikers and equestrians who visit it. Pack out all trash. Leave it clean for the next party to enjoy!

We have hiked this route (without dogs) one summer in July when the temperature at the car was 107 degrees. By the time we reached the cabin at Wiregrass Spring, a great place to watch birds, the temperature had dropped twenty degrees. This area is popular with equestrians and it is not uncommon to see large groups of folks and horses out for a ride.

HIDDEN FOREST TO HAYFORD PEAK

Rating: Strenuous-difficult; trail and cross-country route finding
Recommended for: Well-conditioned dogs, medium-sized and above
Round-trip mileage: 16 miles, 4100' gain; 10-12 hours as dayhike
Recommended as an overnight backpack with camp at Wiregrass Spring
K9 water: NO WATER past Wiregrass Spring; 3-4quart minimum
Ambience: Route through a hidden forest to highest peak in Sheep Range
Best time to hike: April to November

Driving

Maps: Nevada Road & Recreation Atlas, AAA Las Vegas Vicinity Guide

From the junction of I-15 and US-95, take US-95 north to Corn Creek Road and turn right, east. Drive approximately 4.0 miles to the Visitor Center. Just past the Visitor Center, turn left on the Alamo Road and set your odometer to zero. Drive 16.0 miles to Hidden Forest Road and turn right, east. At 19.6 reach the end of the road at a locked gate. This is Deadman Canyon, elevation 5,810'. Park here, careful not to block the gate. High clearance two-wheel drives should be able to make it to the gate.

Hiking

Map: USGS Hayford Peak and Sheep Peak (NV) 7.5-Minute (1:24,000 scale) Quads

Hike up Deadman Canyon five miles to the cabin near Wiregrass Spring. Easily reached within 3.5 hours, this is a great place to spend the night

if planning a two day backpack to climb Hayford. From the cabin, one can either follow the canyon 1.8 miles to a saddle, then up the southwest ridge to the summit of Hayford, or follow the ridge immediately east of the canyon and up Hayford's south ridge. Anticipate 16 miles round trip with 4,100 feet of elevation gain.

Author Andy Zdon on the summit of Hayford Peak
PHOTO: Wynne Benti

Pahranagat National Wildlife Refuge via the Old Road to Alamo
by Florine Lawlor

A paradoxical land lies between the mighty Colorado River and the Spring Mountains of Southern Nevada. Sage, creosote, and mesquite are only a few of the native plants that add a shade of green or silver to the sandy landscape. Like islands in a sea of gray desolation, these oases are utterly incongruous to their surroundings. It is here that flora and fauna flourish in a bewildering variety and luxuriant abundance. Several such beautiful and unspoiled paradises exist on the "Old Road to Alamo."

Travelers speeding past the Desert National Wildlife Refuge sign on US-95 will not be far from the Hidden Forest. Unless specific information regarding its whereabouts has been obtained, such travelers will be unaware that such a fascinating place exists so close to Las Vegas.

At the Corn Creek Station, Desert National Wildlife Refuge sign, a dirt road leaves the main highway and heads eastward toward a high rampart of desert mountains. At first glance, the mountains appear utterly barren and without life. Situated as it is at the foot of the Sheep Mountains, Corn Creek was a natural camping ground for those on their way to Pahranagat Valley and the town of Alamo.

Seed grasses and other edible plants in the sand dunes provided an abundance of food for the early Native Americans. Animals venturing down from the mountains to browse and drink would provide fresh meat, skins, and bone for tools. As mentioned earlier, evidence of prehistoric man can be found around every spring near Corn Creek, while in the foothills of the Sheep Mountains, just above the

A peaceful spot along the trail at Pahranagat Wildlife Refuge PHOTO: Wynne Benti

dunes and springs, is a network of their ancient trails. Some trails lead to nothing, while others lead to seeps of water and sheltered camps once used by these prehistoric travelers.

Leaving Corn Creek, the dirt road forks. We take the left fork, heading northwest past the sign that reads Hidden Forest. Through a maze of cacti and sage, the road ascends a moderate grade and enters a boulder-strewn wash where it winds through a forest of yucca. The desert traveler reaches a narrow portal of rock. It marks the natural boundary of the wonderful arboreal domain lying beyond. The line of demarcation is sharply drawn. To the west extends a vast expanse of desert, ridged, and broken by successive ranges of sterile mountains. To the east, rise the wooded heights of the Sheep Range and the Hidden Forest.

Towering above the Hidden Forest is rugged Hayford Peak (9,912 feet). This remote mountain has long been a favorite with local hikers because of its beautiful scenery along the route to the peak and the spectacular view from its summit.

Passing the Hidden Forest Road (about fifteen miles from Corn Creek Station), the scenery becomes more unusual, isolated, remote. Save for the sighing of the wind and the occasional call of a bird, silence is so complete and unbroken that it makes a profound impression on one whose ears have become accustomed to sounds of human activity. Silhouetted against the sky are twisted yucca and windswept rocky outcrops. Broken, rocky ground stretches from the Sheep Mountains on the east to the Desert Range on the west. Ahead the dirt track stretches invitingly into the vast horizon sometimes disappearing momentarily from view, only to reappear as one travels along.

As White Sage Flat is approached, the landscape begins to flatten. About 5.8 miles north of the turnoff to Hidden Forest, in the bottom of White Sage Flat, there is a branch road leading east and marked with a sign that says White Rock Spring. It is approximately 4.0 miles to the spring area and it makes a lovely hike in the cooler months of the year.

Low, grayish shrubs grow profusely and give the desert floor the appearance of a large billowing dust cloud. At the edge of the flat is a dry lake. This small playa gives evidence of having been at least an occasional camping spot for early Native people. Scattered flint and chert chippings are found along its powdery shoreline. This modem road follows the very same route that was used for untold centuries by game animals and nomadic people to pass back and forth from Pahranagat Valley to the Las Vegas Valley. Precious water sources were found along the way and their locations were remembered for future reference. About 6.2 miles past the White Rock Spring Road, the road forks. The left fork heads west toward Indian Springs along US-95, but this route is forbidden given the presence of a bombing range.

We turn right (north), and passing Dead Horse Ridge and Saddle Mountain of the East Desert Range on the right, the dirt road climbs another series of ridges, crossing Sheep Pass, then drops down into a large valley, surrounded by rugged mountains. A large dry lake bed, its shoreline clustered with clumps of sand dunes, covers two-thirds of the area. This is Cabin Springs Dry Lake which served as an Indian hunting and camping area for centuries.

Once, a violent desert rainstorm took us completely by surprise here. In less than thirty minutes, the bottom of the lake filled with water from shore to shore to a depth of about two feet. As abruptly as it started, the storm blew over. The sun came out and for a short time I got a privileged glimpse back into history when the desert lakes were brimming with water. Within an hour, every trace of the water had retreated into the

Trail along the canal in the Middle Marsh area PHOTO: Wynne Benti

porous earth and the lake bed was again a windswept desert playa.

Sadly, this serene valley was once used as a strafing range. The bullet-riddled wrecks of target automobiles glimmer on the far horizon. Large shell casings and various aircraft debris also litter the ground. Crossing the hard surface of the old lake (be careful here as you don't want to get stuck in the mud), or artfully maneuvering around the east shore of the dry lake, the terrain begins to change. Low hills give way to weathered outcrops of grey rocks, so misshapen that the formations resemble eerie animals. Thousands of erosion holes give the visitor an impression of being watched by myriad owls, hence the name Owl Valley. The road eventually makes its descent into Pahranagat Valley. If it were not for the houses and paved streets which come into view, reality would have been left far behind in this beautiful desert dreamland.

Editor's note: During the summer, the old Road to Alamo is often closed at the Dry Lake, about midway between Corn Creek and Pahranagat due to hazardous conditions on the lake. Closures are marked on either end of the Old Road.

View from fishing pier on Upper Pahranagat Lake   PHOTO: Wynne Benti

BLACK CANYON PETROGLYPHS
PAHRANAGAT NATIONAL WILDLIFE REFUGE

Rating: Easy
Recommended for: All dogs
Round-trip mileage: 0.1 miles, some scrambling, 10 minutes
K9 water: No water; just a short hike from the car; a half quart should do
Ambience: Unusual geometric patterns in the desert varnish on volcanic rock
Best time to hike: Year-round

Driving

Maps: Nevada Road & Recreation Atlas, AAA Las Vegas Vicinity Guide

From the junction of I-15 and US-95, take I-15 north about 21 miles (12.5 miles from 215/I-15) to US-93-Exit 64, the Great Basin Highway, then north on US-93. Reach Pahranagat National Wildlife Refuge sign at 58.6 miles. At approximately 66.9 miles, you'll pass the entrance to

the refuge headquarters on the left. Just about a hundred feet past the road to headquarters, turn right on a dirt road. Park in a little pullout.

Hiking

Maps: USGS Alamo and Alamo SE (NV) 7.5-Minute (1:24,000 scale) Quads

From the car, walk east down the road a few hundred feet, staying left, towards the base of the grey volcanic cliff. Scramble up a footpath through an opening in a fence along the base of the volcanic rock. The path goes just a short distance and deadends, but the presence of the geometrically designed petroglyphs is unlike any that we have seen. Return the same way, or drop down to your right to the big cottonwood in the field below and walk the field back to the car, if it's not wet and muddy.

NORTH MARSH DIKE-UPPER TRAIL LOOP
PAHRANAGAT WILDLIFE REFUGE

Rating: Moderate
Recommended for: Well-conditioned dogs, any size
Mileage: 3.0 miles round-trip, minimal gain, 1.5 hours
K9 water: 2.0 quart minimum; at current low water levels,
lake water is difficult to get to because of soft mud
Posted: Pick up after your dog
Best time to visit: Year-round
Best time to hike: October to May

Driving
Maps: Nevada Road & Recreation Atlas, AAA Las Vegas Vicinity Guide
From the junction of I-15 and US-95, take I-15 north about 21 miles
(12.5 miles from 215/I-15) to US-93-Exit 64, the Great Basin Highway,
then north on US-93 approximately 69.9 miles, 1.5 hours, one-way, to
the entrance to Upper Pahranagat Lake and turn left on a good gravel road that heads back south, between the highway on the east and
the lakes on the west. Drive to a gate, the entrance to the campground. Just past the entrance is a Visitor Center trailer and information kiosk. Turn right and park in the parking area just past the kiosk.

Hiking
Maps: USGS Alamo and Alamo SE (NV) 7.5-Minute (1:24,000 scale) Quads
The hike begins just west of the parking area at the signed North
Marsh Dike. Walk across the tree-lined dike between the North
Marsh and Upper Pahranagat Lake, passing an observation deck in
the center of the dike. On the west shore just follow the signed trail
as it turns south along the lake's western shore. Large dense stands
of cottonwoods and tules line the shore in contrast to the stressed
desert landscape to the west—Joshua trees, yucca, and cholla. At
press time, the lake water level was very low, exposing beaches of fra-
grant, soft, grey mud.

About two miles into the hike, a picnic table beneath the cool
shade of the cottonwoods is reached. Past this, the trail climbs up a
short knoll and continues south past a telescope and benches. While

Pahranagat Wildlife Refuge is a lush oasis amidst Nevada's basin and range with excellent viewing of wildlife including native and migratory birds. PHOTO: Wynne Benti

egrets and blue heron stroll in the lake waters, turkey vultures soar in a relentless circle just over the brown desert to the west. The trail is shadeless along this stretch until it turns east again at the bottom of the lake. Pass a beautiful wood fishing pier which also houses the outtake valve to the lower lakes. In autumn, the pom-poms of the rabbitbrush growing along the southern edge of the lake are huge and bright golden yellow.The cottonwood leaves turn gold not long after the rabbitbrush begins to fade. The trail passes through the campground then follows the gravel road back up to the parking area. Leash your dog along the road here as cars do access the parking lot.

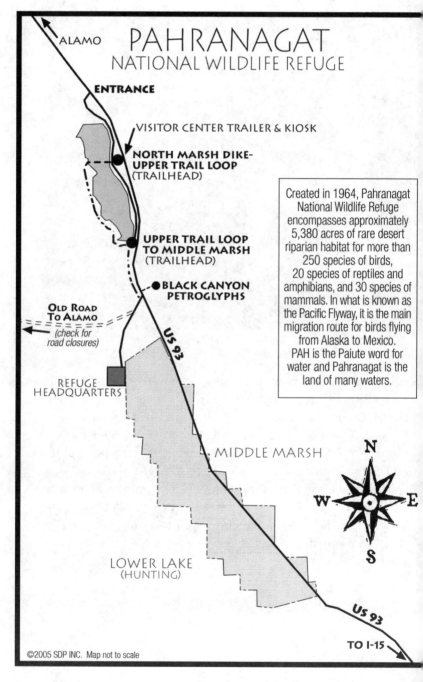

PAHRANAGAT
NATIONAL WILDLIFE REFUGE

ALAMO

ENTRANCE

VISITOR CENTER TRAILER & KIOSK

NORTH MARSH DIKE-UPPER TRAIL LOOP
(TRAILHEAD)

UPPER TRAIL LOOP TO MIDDLE MARSH
(TRAILHEAD)

● BLACK CANYON PETROGLYPHS

OLD ROAD TO ALAMO
(check for road closures)

REFUGE HEADQUARTERS

US 93

MIDDLE MARSH

LOWER LAKE
(HUNTING)

US 93

TO I-15

Created in 1964, Pahranagat National Wildlife Refuge encompasses approximately 5,380 acres of rare desert riparian habitat for more than 250 species of birds, 20 species of reptiles and amphibians, and 30 species of mammals. In what is known as the Pacific Flyway, it is the main migration route for birds flying from Alaska to Mexico. PAH is the Paiute word for water and Pahranagat is the land of many waters.

N
W E
S

UPPER TRAIL LOOP TO MIDDLE MARSH
PAHRANAGAT NATIONAL WILDLIFE REFUGE

Rating: Easy-moderate
Recommended for: Well-conditioned dogs, any size
Mileage: 2.0 miles round-trip, 40 minutes
K9 water: Water; 1.0 quart minimum
Posted: Pick up after your dog
Best time to visit: Year-round
Best time to hike: October to May

Driving
Maps: Nevada Road & Recreation Atlas, AAA Las Vegas Vicinity Guide
From the junction of I-15 and US-95, take I-15 north about 21 miles
(12.5 miles from 215/I-15) to US-93-Exit 64, the Great Basin Highway,
then north on US-93 approximately 69.9 miles, 1.5 hours, one-way, to
the entrance to Upper Pahranagat Lake and turn left on a good gravel road. Drive 2.4 miles to the end of the campground and park careful not to block the locked gate (Upper Loop Trail).

Hiking
Maps: USGS Alamo and Alamo SE (NV) 7.5-Minute (1:24,000 scale) Quads
From the parking area, hike past the locked gate to the fishing pier
and turn left, down a flight of concrete steps. This is a beautiful segment of the trail beneath the cottonwoods, follows the drainage canal
to the lower lakes. Stay right at a fork (left goes back to the car). The
trail crosses the ditch and follows the west side (shadeless in afternoon) for awhile, then crosses back east towards the highway again
at a large fork. Put leashes on here, as you will be turning right at the
stop sign just before the highway. The trail continues beneath the
highway to the refuge headquarters road and sign. You can turn
around here or wander down to the refuge headquarters or out along
the dikes of Middle Marsh.

CALICO BASIN AND VICINITY

The Old Spanish Trail, the main route from Santa Fe to the Pueblo of Los Angeles passed by Calico Basin with its hidden springs and brilliantly colored red and tan sandstone formations, and continued on past Red Rock and Blue Diamond. Prehistoric ancestors of the Southern Paiute lived in the region 10-12,000 years ago and more recently, the Southern Paiute, who vanished from the scene by the early 20th century.

When Europeans started coming through on the trail, so began the enslavement of the Southern Paiutes. The Paiutes were farmers and did not ride horses. The Western Utes, the Spanish, the New Mexican traders and American trappers traveled through the homeland of the Southern Paiutes on horseback, ambushing and taking slaves when the Paiutes went to get water at the precious springs along the trail. Smaller groups of Paiutes lost more than half of their women and children to slavery. In one instance, a desperate mother recaptured her stolen child only to be cornered by angry slavers wanting the baby back. Instead of acquiescing, she threw the baby to its death over a cliff.

Reports surfaced about Paiute camps of all men, with no women or children. With the arrival of Mormons in Southern Nevada, slavery of the Paiutes subsided somewhat as neither Mormons nor Utah Territorial Law tolerated the practice of human bondage. The influx of Mormons and their new ever-expanding settlements permanently displaced the Paiutes across Southern Nevada. Their numbers decreased drastically as they died out. In 1848 California and New Mexico became U.S. Territories and abolished slavery. Even so, the practice continued along the Old Spanish Trail until the traders from New Mexico and other areas stopped using the trail.

Gated road at beginning of the hike PHOTO: Wynne Benti

THE CCC CATCH BASINS

Access to this area in recent years due to private property issues has become increasingly difficult. Sadly, between scouting the trail and publication, access to the powerline road (alternate route) was terminated by Summerlin developers who posted a no trespassing sign. They are blocking access to your public lands! Also during this time, the primary access route in from SR-159 was bladed and made practically inaccessible to vehicles. You may have to park at the highway and walk in, adding an additional 10 miles to the hike resulting in a rating of strenuous.

Rating: Moderate
Recommended for: Well-conditioned dogs, any size
Round-trip mileage from the gate: 3.0 miles, 80' gain. 1-2 hours
Round-trip mileage from SR-159: 12.2 miles, 300' gain; 5-6 hours
K9 water: Water; 2-quart minimum (4-quarts from the highway)
Recommended: Pets on leash. Clean up after your pet. No facilities.
Ambience: Stark beauty of a classic desert wash
Best time to hike: November to April. Wash subject to flash floods.
Hiking from highway:
Map: Nevada Road & Recreation Atlas, AAA Las Vegas Vicinity Guide
From the intersection of the 215-Western Beltway and SR-159/West

CCC Tank 1 PHOTO: Wynne Benti

Charleston Blvd., drive west on SR-159 approximately 1.7 miles. Turn right on a dirt track through a break in a wall of boulders, marked by a sign that says "no trespassing, private property" which is odd because it's posted on public land. Note the shooting range across the road (for a landmark on the return trip). If the road is accessible, set your odometer to zero. Just before press time the road was bladed and access made practically impossible. If this is the case, park off the road and hike in from this point.

There was a land dispute concerning this access route between the private property owners, the BLM and the public who were shut out by the developers in 1998. From SR-159, note pole lines in the distance. A road follows the pole lines from Summerlin to Calico Basin, but that alternate access point to Brownstone was just terminated by the posting of private property signs.

From SR-159, either drive or walk the dirt track. It turns right, and backtracks a few hundred feet toward Summerlin then:

0.1   Cross an east-west trending wash

0.2   Out of the wash and on to a two track that heads up a north-south trending wash, paralleling the pole line on the right

0.7   Cross under the pole line (the alternate route coming in from Summerlin, if the development doesn't totally close it off) and continue straight up canyon. Stay left at all forks. Just head towards the big canyon, Brownstone, ahead of you.

4.6   Locked gate—park

Hiking

Map: USGS La Madre Mountain (NV) 7.5-Minute (1:24,000 scale) Quad

From the locked gate, hike north up the left side of the wash about a quarter-mile to a shallow gully in the sandstone. Watch for scrub live oak against the base of the sandstone and listen for birds. At the head of the gully a concrete catch basin can be seen, the first of two such water basins built by the Civilian Conservation Corps (CCC) during the 1930s. Look across the wash to the red hills up the canyon, our second destination. Walk the easiest route up the wash, mostly left/center. Eventually, you'll come upon an old Jeep track, that is followed up the wash, in the general direction of the red hills on the east side, keeping right at forks. Note the

Looking west across CCC Tank II to Turtlehead Peak   PHOTO: Wynne Benti

backside of Turtlehead Peak on the west. The track takes you to the second CCC concrete catch basin nestled in the red sandstone cliffs east of Turtlehead. Return the way you came. The more adventurous can pick a return route through the red cliffs.

Notes

Previously named Solomon Canyon after Dewey Solomon who discovered it in the 1930s, Brownstone Canyon is on the National Register of Historic Places. Used primarily as a camp by prehistoric people almost 12,000 years ago, agave roasting pits are hidden beneath oaks in the canyon.

In March 1933, U.S. President Franklin Delano Roosevelt proposed to recruit thousands of unemployed men and put them to work saving the country's natural resources from destruction.

Approved by Congress, over the duration of the CCC's existence, more than 600,000 men and women enrolled and were sent to work across the country. The work of the CCC from nearly seventy years ago, can be seen all over Las Vegas and the surrounding backcountry.

Flash flood warning!

The entire wash is subject to flash floods especially in summer.

Archaeological sites are protected by federal law

Archaeological sites and artifacts are protected by the Antiquities Act of 1906 and the Archaeological Resources Protection Act of 1979. Historic and prehistoric sites on federal lands are protected and defacement, removal, excavation or destruction of such antiquities is prohibited by law.

ASSISI CANYON TO ASH CREEK SPRING

Rating: Easy
Recommended for: All dogs
Round-trip mileage: 1.5 miles, 1 hour
K9 water: Seasonal water in Ash Spring; 1 quart minimum
Posted: Pets on leash. Clean up after your pet. No facilities.
Ambience: Meandering trail along the red Calico Hills to meadow
Best time to hike: Year-round with a very early morning start in summer.

Driving

Maps: Nevada Road & Recreation Atlas, AAA Las Vegas Vicinity Guide

From the intersection of the 215-Western Beltway and 159/West Charleston Blvd., drive west on 159. Turn left on the signed Calico Basin Road. Drive 1.2 miles to Calico Drive and turn right. In 0.1 mile, turn left on Assisi Canyon. Note the flood destruction in the wash to the left. Park at the corner of Assisi and Sandstone. The trail starts on the west end of Sandstone Drive, on the north side of the gate.

Hiking

Map: USGS La Madre Mountain (NV) 7.5-Minute (1:24,000 scale) Quad

Follow the wide trail past the gate across a shallow wash toward the red Calico hills, and what appears to be a dead-end gully. Actually, at the very top of this steep gully is the Calico Tank. Just before the big rock at the mouth of the gully, the trail forks right and follows the base of the hills above Calico Basin. To your right are the residential homes of Calico Basin. You'll pass blank wood posts, once markers for an interpretive trail associated with the now abandoned BLM picnic area, on your right. Soon a monstrous and eerie concrete foundation for something huge and never finished comes into view below the trail. There are several of these mysterious, partially built projects scattered across Calico Basin—big dreams built with big money that evaporated somewhere along the way. The trail passes by the concrete foundation, and then drops down behind it into a wide spring fed wash with sandy red soils, lush grasses and desert willows with orchid-like blossoms in late July-early August. This is Ash Creek Spring (seasonal). Turn left and wander up into the meadow beneath the

Ash Creek Spring PHOTO: Wynne Benti

shade (late spring through autumn) of the cottonwoods. The dogs will have a wonderful time playing in the water and the lush meadow.

Notes

Please respect all no trespassing signs and private property boundaries in Calico Basin. This area has many wonderful meandering walks, that are easy to do once you become familiar with the terrain.

About forty years ago, some friends were offered a five acre parcel with a house for $27,000 in Calico Basin. Now a five acre parcel with a house runs $2.5 million and up. Once miles from the Las Vegas city limits, Calico Basin was best known for its preponderance of colorful desert rats, hermits and folk who liked to take pot shots at visitors with shotguns filled with rock salt. With the escalation of real estate prices and expansion of Vegas into public lands, Calico Basin has since become quite gentrified. Most of the old desert rats moved out long ago, but their legacy continues, somewhat ironically, in the form of posted signs and lots of chain link fences reminding visitors that Calico Basin is a residential neighborhood and not a recreation area.

CALICO BASIN TO SANDSTONE QUARRY

Rating: Moderately-strenuous, trail, some cross-country with route-finding
Recommended for: Well-conditioned dogs
Round-trip mileage: 3.5 miles, 860' gain. 3-4 hours
K9 water: Seasonal spring water in Gateway Canyon; 2-3 quart minimum
Posted: Pets on leash. Clean up after your pet. No facilities.
Ambience: From one beautiful basin to another with spectacular scenery!
Best time to hike: November-April. Get an early morning start.

Driving
Maps: Nevada Road & Recreation Atlas, AAA Las Vegas Vicinity Guide

From the intersection of the 215-Western Beltway and 159/West Charleston Blvd., drive west on 159. Drive 3.4 miles to Calico Basin Road and turn right. Drive 1.2 miles to Calico Drive and turn right. At 1.3 miles turn left on Assisi Canyon. Drive about 0.1 miles to Sandstone drive and turn right. Drive to the east end of the road and park, careful not to block any driveways.

Hiking
Map: USGS La Madre Mountain (NV) 7.5-Minute (1:24,000 scale) Quad

From the end of Sandstone Drive, walk north on a road easement in between private property fencelines, noted by a large dirt berm between it and the street. The key in Calico Basin is not to cross private property. Follow the well-worn footpath down and across a wide steep wash, due north toward the golden-red hills on the other side of the wash. Here, the last pole on a powerline will come into view. Head for that last pole. When you reach the last pole, turn left, west, paralleling a chain link fence that eventually ends. Keep walking straight west, crossing a shallow wash marked by wood posts until you pick up a Jeep trail. Turn right following the Jeep trail, northeasterly, paralleling the hills on your right, east. Continue on the old Jeep trail as it merges with an unmarked well-worn use trail that climbs a moderately steep hill to a saddle (or pass) between points 4987' and 4714' on your USGS La Madre Mountain Quad or Green Trails map. It's about three-quarter mile from the car to this point. You can see Turtlehead Peak to the north.

Follow the old Jeep trail from last power pole. PHOTO: Wynne Benti

Over the pass the trail swings left, sidehilling for about a quarter-mile then drops down into the wash below you. Follow the wash in the direction of Turtlehead Peak. This is Gateway Canyon.

In August of 2005, there was plenty of water in the wash, but it is seasonal. This somewhat shaded location in the creek with its plentiful water (depending on the year) is a great destination in itself. Some hikers and their canine companions may wish to stop here and make this point the end of the hike. There are plenty of spots to explore with cool spring water.

Continue scrambling up the wash. Not far from the lush overgrowth of the lower creek, a 15-foot high water-worn waterfall spans the wash. The trail goes up the left side of the waterfall. Scramble up and over the waterfall. Walking up the wash just a short way, turn left, west, into a shallow canyon that takes you to the backside of the Calico Hills, which can be soon be seen from within the canyon.

The trail meanders from side to side in the small canyon, then as

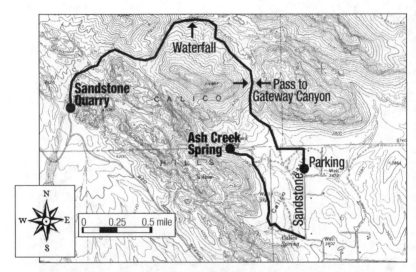

the canyon broadens out just before reaching the hills, the trail turns right, north. Walk about 0.1 mile, passing some lovely shade trees, then turn left, west, down into the golden-colored sandstone of the Calico Hills. Pick you way through the sandstone on the use-trail

Bypass the waterfall on the left PHOTO: Wynne Benti

another 0.1 mile to the Calico Tanks Trail. Turn right on the Calico Tanks Trail (trail marker) and follow the wash out, then west to the Sandstone Quarry. Return by the same route or pick up the second car if doing it as a car shuttle.

Alternate hiking return route:

From Sandstone Quarry take the signed Calico Hills Trail on the south side of the parking lot back to Calico Basin. Follow the trail south almost to the entrance station and turn left, over the hill at the base of the red cliffs to Red Springs, through the neighborhood to your car at Sandstone Drive.

The trail from the pass parallels wash then drops down into it heading
towards Turtlehead Peak PHOTO: Wynne Benti

Red Springs Boardwalk

Rating: Super-easy
Recommended for: Small, out-of-shape or older dogs
Round-trip mileage: 0.5 miles, flat, 30 minutes
K9 water: Water; 1-quart minimum
Posted: Pets on leash. Clean up after your pet. No facilities.
Ambience: Beautifully engineered boardwalk above natural springs
Best time to hike: November-April. Get an early morning start.

Driving

Maps: Nevada Road & Recreation Atlas, AAA Las Vegas Vicinity Guide

From the intersection of the 215-Western Beltway and 159/West Charleston Blvd., drive west on 159. Drive 3.4 miles to Calico Basin Road and turn right. Continue 1.2 miles to Calico Drive and the entrance to Red Springs Picnic Area.

Walk

At the time we scouted Red Springs, the area was not yet officially open as a park, and no note as to whether or not dogs would be allowed. The boardwalk is beautifully engineered to protect the frag-

Megan on the boardwalk. Turtlehead on the horizon. PHOTO: Wynne Benti

ile spring and riparian area. Just follow the boardwalk up and around a lovely desert riparian habitat and spring with beautiful views of Calico Basin. Canopied benches provide a peaceful place to sit. We used to start the Calico Basin route to Sandstone Quarry from this old picnic area, but new fences have blocked off access. At press time, the picnic are was closed for restoration and it wasn't clear whether or not it would be open to dogs, but there are plenty of places to walk your dogs as described earlier off Assisi.

Red Rock

Red Rock National Conservation Area (NCA) is perhaps one of the most beautiful desert places in the United States, certainly in Southern Nevada. One of the unique gems of the BLM's land holdings, its spectacular sandstone cliffs and wide open desert terrain are just a stone's throw away from the edge of Summerlin. But it wasn't always like that. Sadly, the BLM sold more than 100,000 acres of public lands for development at the edge of Red Rock and Kyle Canyon. Not even a decade ago, Red Rock was more isolated than it is now.

TRAILS

The trails in Red Rock are well-planned, signed and easy to follow, ranking as one of the best trail systems in the country for clarity of hiking information. Most of the trailheads have restrooms, detailed interpretive information, plastic canine waste bags for on the trail, trash and recycling receptacles. The people of Las Vegas love and cherish all of their parks, but especially this one. Most these amenities were paid for with donations from the community.

FEE AREA & LATE EXIT PERMITS

The Red Rock Scenic Loop Road is currently open 6am to 5pm in winter and 6am to 8pm in summer (hours are subject to change and the road is subject to fire and weather closure). There is a fee to enter Red Rock and drive the scenic route. At press time, once the entrance station closes (at 4:30pm), the fee is waived. As long as the gate is open, access is available, which is great for late afternoon hikes in summer. If your car is parked at one of the trailheads along the scenic drive outside the posted hours you may be fined and ticketed. If you know you won't be back to your vehicle before the main gate closes, you can request a FREE *Late Exit Permit* by calling 702-515-5050 and leaving a message with your name, vehicle make, and trailhead information, no later than 4p.m. on the day of your hike.

WEATHER

Since Red Rock's elevation is higher than Las Vegas, year-round temperatures are up to ten degrees cooler or more depending on the location—the Visitor Center is 3,720 feet while the high point, Mt. Wilson, is 7,070 feet.

Summer hikes started at dawn or a few hours before sunset can be very pleasant. We hike the west side trails (Pine Creek, First Creek, etc.) in the evening and east side (Calico Hills) in morning when we can take full advantage of the sun's low position on the horizon.

There is nothing quite like a summer evening hike on the west side trails following an afternoon thunderstorm. The rain cools down the sandstone which, having been in the sun all day, has absorbed the day's heat. As a side note, very intense summer thunderstorms can cause flash flooding in the washes and canyons.

Winter finds snow at the higher elevations in the La Madre Mountain Wilderness Area, the peaks surrounding the Red Rock basin. Heavy winter snow in the La Madres makes for heavy runoff in surrounding washes and canyons. Many of the backcountry routes have are washed out from time to time by this winter runoff. Certain canyons are subject to larger amounts of runoff than others.

ROAD CLOSURES AND BACKCOUNTRY RESCUES

The BLM posts road closures at the Red Rock entrance station so keep your eye open for a piece of paper taped to the fee station window.

If you break down on a backcountry route or get stranded somewhere, be prepared for the worst case scenario. General rule of thumb is to stay with the vehicle as a car is easier to find than a person wandering the desert. If you decide to walk out, be prepared with water and extra food in your daypack; know how far you'll have to walk to get back to a main road.

Long before cell phones were invented, when the scenic drive through Red Rock was dirt, Jim Lawlor Sr. drove his Chevy Malibu all the way to Pahrump via the Old Potato Pass Road (now the Rocky Gap 4x4 Road). The Lawlor family probably walked out of more sticky situations than anyone else we know. Florine Lawlor and friend Leslie Payne once hiked 27 miles back to pavement in their "flip-flops." It makes all the difference to be traveling with a friend. Those long walks back to civilization are much more enjoyable.

If you travel any road closed by the BLM and get stuck or break down, they will not come get you. Red Rock National Conservation Area generally does not handle rescue operations, human or otherwise. A trapped vehicle is completely your responsibility to get out. All rescues in Clark County are supervised by the Las Vegas Metropolitan Police Department's Search and Rescue unit and are initiated by calling 911.

CELL PHONE RECEPTION (OR LACK THEREOF)

With Summerlin only a few miles away, cell reception shouldn't be a problem—right? Think again! Those mesas, and walls of sandstone, then limestone create a pretty formidable barrier to any cell phone reception in Red Rock, unless you happen to be at the Visitor Center. We tried to make cell phone calls from the summit of North Peak looking out over Red Rock, and from the top of Brownstone Canyon, both with a straight visible line to the Strip. We were only able to get through to 911 and no other numbers.

MOENKOPI LOOP

Rating: Easy
Recommended for: Small, out-of-shape or older dogs
Round-trip mileage: 2.0 mile round-trip, 1 hour
K9 water: No water; 2-quart minimum
Posted: Pets on leash. Clean up after your pet.
Ambience: Meandering hike around the BLM Visitor Center
Best time to hike: November to April.
Early morning or late afternoon start any other time of the year.

Driving
Maps: Nevada Road & Recreation Atlas, AAA Las Vegas Vicinity Guide

From the intersection of the 215-Western Beltway and 159/West Charleston Blvd., drive west on SR-159 approximately 5.2 miles to the entrance for the Red Rock Scenic Drive/BLM Visitor Center and turn right. From the entrance station take the left driveway to the Visitor Center. Restrooms, pay phones, vending machines, picnic tables and a neat desert tortoise habitat at the Visitor Center.

Hiking
Map: Green Trails Maps-Red Rock NCA #2474S

From the parking lot, walk toward the Visitor Center entrance. Look for the Moenkopi trail sign off to the left. The trail provides a great overview of Red Rock, the bright red Calico Hills to the east and the sandstone cliffs to the west.

Hiking
Unfortunately, a lightning strike in July 2005 burned most of the area around this trail. The yuccas are now just scorched black silhouettes against the red rock of the Calico Hills. Summer monsoons in August brought some wildflowers with more to come after winter.

Calico Hills Trail

Rating: Moderate
Recommended for: Well-conditioned dogs, any size
Round-trip mileage: Varies by access point. Up to 3.6 miles one-way. Can be done in 2.0 mile round-trip segments from various pints along the Scenic Loop Road.
K9 water: No water; 2-quarts minimum
Posted: Pets on leash. Clean up after your pet.
Ambience: Hike along a scenic escarpment right along the bright red sandstone base of the Calico Hills.
Best time to hike: November to April. Start early morning or late afternoon other times of the year. Seasonal water in wash.

Driving
Maps: Nevada Road & Recreation Atlas, AAA Las Vegas Vicinity Guide
From the intersection of the 215-Western Beltway and 159/West Charleston Blvd., drive west on SR-159 approximately 5.2 miles to the entrance for the Red Rock Scenic Drive/BLM Visitor Center and turn right. Just past the entrance station is a parking area. The trail starts behind the yellow pedestrian sign just to the east and across the street from the parking area.

Hiking
Maps: USGS La Madre Mountain (NV) 7.5-Minute (1:24,000 scale) Quad; Green Trails Maps-Red Rock NCA #2474S
The Calico Hills Trail trail starts just past the Red Rock NCA entrance station to Sandstone Quarry and can be done from either end. It can be followed from here in one long segment, 3.6 miles one-way northwest to the Sandstone Quarry Trailhead, or broken up into much shorter segments about a mile one-way each. If you have the luxury of two cars, leave one car at Sandstone Quarry and start at the beginning of the Calico Hills Trail just behind the entrance station. Then you don't have to walk back. There is seasonal water in narrow wash between the trail and the hills, but don't count on it.

Park behind the fee station. The trail starts at pedestrian sign right across from the parking area. It crosses open rolling yucca desert then

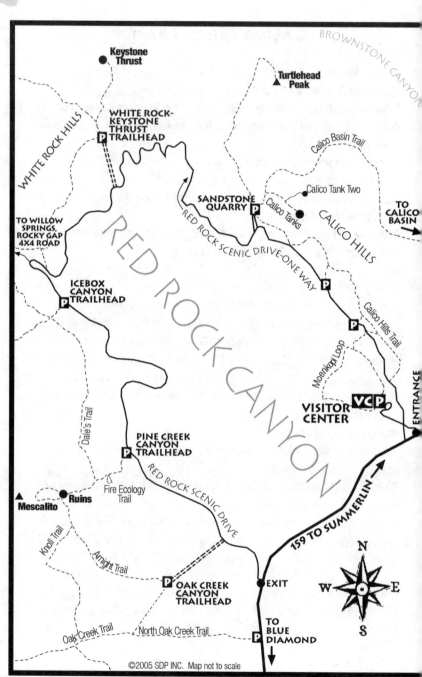

©2005 SDP INC. Map not to scale

Dogs a-plenty on the Calico Tanks Trail PHOTO: Wynne Benti

drops down into the narrow wash between the magnificent red Calico Hills and the scenic drive. The trail sidehills just above the wash and across from the beautiful bright red Calico Hills. It's a great bugseye view of the red hills—they are right there spread before you in all their vivid splendor! In the late afternoon, the color of the red hills are intensified by the western sun.

The area between the Visitor Center, the Calico Hills and almost all the way to Sandstone Quarry were burned by a lightning-strike fire in July 2005. Look for a cropping of new grasses in the area. The yucca and cacti will take much longer to come back.

CALICO HILLS TRAIL SYSTEM

Mileages rom the parking are behind the entrance station

Visitor Center:	1.5 miles easy
Calico I:	1.1 miles easy
Calico II:	2.0 miles moderate
Sandstone Quarry:	3.6 miles moderate

CALICO TANKS TRAIL

Rating: Easy-Moderate
Recommended for: Well-conditioned dogs, any size
Round-trip mileage: 3.0 miles, 400' of gain, 1-2 hours on trail, wash then up the red sandstone of the Chinle Formation, into the heart of the Calico Hills
K9 water: No water on trail; 1-quart minimum; seasonal water in sandstone waterpockets (filled with little black tadpoles in midsummer)
Posted: Pets on leash. Clean up after your pet.
Ambience: Hike deep within the red and yellow sandstone hills
Lots of dogs on weekends. Great hike for every member of the family!
Best time to hike: Year-round. Get an early morning start in summer.

Driving

Maps: Nevada Road & Recreation Atlas, AAA Las Vegas Vicinity Guide
From the Red Rock NCA entrance station, drive about 2.8 miles to the parking area for the Sandstone Quarry Trailhead. Restrooms.

Hiking

*Maps: USGS La Madre Mountain (NV) 7.5-Minute (1:24,000 scale) Quad;
Green Trails Maps-Red Rock NCA #2474S*

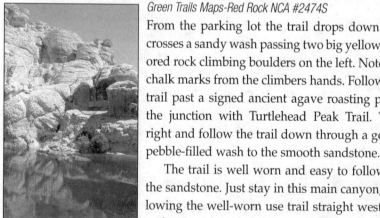

From the parking lot the trail drops down and crosses a sandy wash passing two big yellow-colored rock climbing boulders on the left. Note the chalk marks from the climbers hands. Follow the trail past a signed ancient agave roasting pit to the junction with Turtlehead Peak Trail. Turn right and follow the trail down through a gentle pebble-filled wash to the smooth sandstone.

The trail is well worn and easy to follow on the sandstone. Just stay in this main canyon, following the well-worn use trail straight west, up and across the white sandstone cliffs to a large, steep-walled water tank, inaccessible to all but the most experienced climbers. There is a little scrambling to get to the main tank overlook. The views are beautiful down into the red cliffs of Calico Basin to the south.

Rosy at Calico Tank Two with Turtlehead Peak behind. PHOTO: Wynne Benti

CALICO TANK TWO
(OPTIONAL SPUR HIKE TO ANOTHER TANK)

Rating: Moderate, some Class 2 scrambling up a steep, loose gully
Recommended for: Well-conditioned dogs, any size
Round-trip mileage: 3.0 miles, 400' of gain, 1-2 hours on trail, wash then up the red and gold sandstone into the heart of the Calico Hills
K9 water: No water on trail; 1-quart minimum; seasonal water in sandstone waterpockets (tadpoles in midsummer).
Posted: Pets on leash. Clean up after your pet.
Ambience: Lovely walk and scramble for hearty souls with good balance
Best time to hike: Year-round. Get an early morning start in summer.

Driving
Maps: Nevada Road & Recreation Atlas, AAA Las Vegas Vicinity Guide
From the Red Rock NCA entrance station, drive about 2.8 miles to the parking area for the Sandstone Quarry Trailhead. Restrooms.

Hiking
Maps: USGS La Madre Mountain (NV) 7.5-Minute (1:24,000 scale) Quad;
Green Trails Maps-Red Rock NCA #2474S
From the parking lot the trail drops down and crosses a sandy wash passing two big yellow-colored rock climbing boulders on the left. Note the chalk marks from the climbers hands. Follow the trail past a signed ancient agave roasting pit to the junction with Turtlehead Peak Trail. Turn right and follow the trail down through a gentle pebble-filled wash to smooth sandstone. The trail is well worn and easy to follow on the sandstone. Stay far left on a series of steps and ducks which take you to a small seasonal waterpocket. The main Calico Tanks Trail continues straight ahead. Look left for a steep narrow gully against a white wall of sandstone. Climb this steep, loose gully to what appears to be a deadend at an impassable wall, then walk left to easier footing. The route over the wall should become apparent. Drop down and turn right again heading west. Careful walking and you will come upon a wonderful natural water tank with its own little fragile ecosystem. Do not let dogs pollute this or any other precious desert waterpocket. The views of Turtlehead Peak from this spot are fabulous.

Turtlehead Peak Trail

Rating: Very Strenuous
Recommended for: Well-conditioned dogs, any size
Round-trip mileage: 5.0 miles round-trip, 2043' of gain, 3-4 hours
K9 water: No water; 2-4 quarts minimum
Posted: Pets on leash. Clean up after your pet.
Ambience: Hike up a geological landmark
Best time to hike: November to April. Get an early morning start.

Driving

Maps: Nevada Road & Recreation Atlas, AAA Las Vegas Vicinity Guide

From the Red Rock NCA entrance station, drive about 2.8 miles to the parking area for the Sandstone Quarry Trailhead.

Hiking

Maps: USGS La Madre Mountain (NV) 7.5-Minute (1:24,000 scale) Quad;
Green Trails Maps-Red Rock NCA #2474S

Turtlehead is the neat looking peak on the low skyline behind the

Megan and Ginger on Turtlehead Peak.
PHOTO: Jim Lawlor

Calico Hills. From the parking lot, follow the trail as it drops down and crosses a sandy wash, passing two big yellow rock climbing boulders on the left. Note the chalk marks from the climbers hands. Follow the trail past a signed ancient agave roasting pit to the junction with Calico Tanks (signed). Take the left fork. Follow the trail over a rise, then in and out of a wash continuing along the northwest side of Turtlehead. Follow the well-worn use trail up the steep, loose gully northwest of the peak to the summit ridge. Continue on the rugged ridge to the summit. This is a steep sucker of a trail not for the faint of heart and should be only done in cool weather. It's a short,

Summer thunderstorms around Turtlehead Peak   PHOTO: Wynne Benti

steep workout.

We hiked this peak once in April and saw a half dozen rattlesnakes. They were however, they seemed rather lethargic, barely rattling their tails. Don't be fooled, they move fast even in a semi-hibernation state. Most of the time, we don't see any snakes.

Turtlehead can also be climbed from Brownstone Canyon on the backside as long as road access is available to the public.

Keystone Thrust Trail

Rating: Moderate
Recommended for: Well-conditioned dogs, any size
Round-trip mileage: 2.6 miles, 360' of gain, 1-1.5 hours
K9 water: No water; 2-quarts minimum
Posted: Pets on leash. Clean up after your pet.
Ambience: Geology field-trip to a thrust fault where Bonanza King limestone meets Aztec sandstone
Best time to hike: November to April. Get an early morning start in summer.

Driving
Maps: Nevada Road & Recreation Atlas, AAA Las Vegas Vicinity Guide
From the Red Rock NCA entrance station drive, about 6.0 miles to a gravel road signed White Rock Spring Trailhead. Turn right and go 0.8 miles to the Keystone Thrust trailhead. Restrooms.

Hiking
Maps: USGS La Madre Mountain (NV) 7.5-Minute (1:24,000 scale) Quad;
Green Trails Maps-Red Rock NCA #2474S
From the parking lot follow the trail north passing the interpretive sign for the ancient agave pit. The trail crosses a wash (don't walk up the wash) and turns hard right at the junction with the White Rock Loop Trail and climbs a short set of stairs. Immediately you be treated beautiful expansive view across Red Rock.

Follow an old two-track jeep trail up an undulating hill to a fork marked by an arrow pointing back the way you came. The fork to the right drops down to the wash. Looking down into the wash you can see the grey and pink rock. The grey rock, known as Bonanza King Formation was deposited 540 million years ago during the Paleozoic Era. These grey older rocks, a combination of limestone and dolomite, sit on top of the younger pink rocks or Aztec Sandstone deposited 206 million years ago during the Jurassic Period. Younger rocks on top of older rocks is not how rocks are normally deposited. Instead, it indicates the present of a major thrust fault that is the result of major compression deep within the Earth's crust. This thrust fault is known as the Wilson Cliffs thrust. The shallow wash is inviting

Rosy admires the juxtaposition of the grey Bonanza King formation with the pink
Aztec Sandstone just off the Keystone Thrust Trail PHOTO: Wynne Benti

with its ducks marking the supposed trail, but a hidden 30-40 foot
waterfall is an obstacle to anyone but the rock climbers. Often the
wash is moistened by winter showers and spring runoff through
April. On wet years, there is water in the waterpockets through summer when small black tadpoles can also be observed.

White Rock-La Madre Springs Loop

Rating: Moderate-strenuous
Recommended for: Well-conditioned dogs, any size
Round-trip mileage: 5.8 miles round-trip, 400' of gain, 4-5 hours
K9 water: No water; 3-quarts minimum
Posted: Pets on leash. Clean up after your pet.
Ambience: Trail meanders around the White Rock Hills, through Willow Springs, then along the rolling desert plateau.
Best time to hike: Year-round. Get an early morning start in summer.

Driving

Maps: Nevada Road & Recreation Atlas, AAA Las Vegas Vicinity Guide

From the Red Rock NCA entrance station, drive 6.0 miles to a gravel road signed White Rock Spring Trailhead. Turn right and go 0.8 miles to the trailhead. Restrooms.

Hiking

Maps: USGS La Madre Mountain (NV) 7.5-Minute (1:24,000 scale) Quad;
Green Trails Maps-Red Rock NCA #2474S

From the parking lot follow the trail north about 0.2 miles to 4,960' and a fork, the junction with the Keystone Thrust Trail. Take the left fork as it climbs almost 1,000 feet along the side of point 8,977'. Follow this 2.4 miles to the intersection with the La Madre Springs Trail. If you were to go right at this junction add another 1.5 miles one-way to the end of the La Madre Springs Trail. We are going to turn left at this junction, heading southwest 0.6 miles to elevation 4,760' and another fork. To the right (west) is the Rocky Gap 4x4 Road. Head left, southeast 0.8 miles to the Willow Springs Picnic Area. Walk through the picnic area and continue south about 0.9 miles to elevation 4,520' and a fork, the junction with the Grand Circle Loop. Stay left on the White Rock trail and follow it north back 1.7 miles to the parking lot and trailhead.

La Madre Springs Trail

Rating: Moderate
Recommended for: Well-conditioned dogs, any size
Round-trip mileage: 4.2 miles, 520' gain from junction of La Madre Springs Trail and the Rocky Gap 4x4 Road; add 1.6 miles rt, 100' gain from the Willow Springs parking area, 2-3 hours
K9 water: No water on trail; 2-quarts minimum; water at spring
Posted: Pets on leash. Clean up after your pet.
Ambience: Peaceful walk along the backside of the White Rock Hills
Best time to hike: November to April. Get an early morning start.

Driving

Maps: Nevada Road & Recreation Atlas, AAA Las Vegas Vicinity Guide

From the Red Rock NCA entrance station, drive 7.3 miles on the scenic loop to the paved White Rock Loop Road. Turn right and drive 0.7 miles to the end of the paved road at Willow Springs Picnic Area, the beginning of the unmaintained Rocky Gap 4x4 Road (two-wheel drive cars park here in the parking area). Four-wheel drives continue up the gravel road to the signed trailhead at 0.8 miles on the right (just across the rugged wash). Road conditions can change at any time. This road is posted by the BLM as unmaintained/travel at your own risk, so if you get you car stuck, be prepared to extract it at your own expense!

Hiking

Maps: USGS La Madre Mountain (NV) 7.5-Minute (1:24,000 scale) Quad;
Green Trails Maps-Red Rock NCA #2474S

From the parking area at Willow Spring, hike up the Rocky Gap Road about 0.8 to the signed trailhead on the right. Turn right, north, and walk up the trail which provides an excellent view of the great White Rock Hills across the wash.

The trail maintains a steady gain of elevation. As you near the springs, you'll pass through a large stand of junipers. They are so are neatly arranged they look as if someone planted them. Between the junipers are a few old concrete pads where the Civilian Conservation

Rosy cools off in La Madre Spring one early August morning PHOTO: Wynne Benti

Trail to La Madre Springs and backside of the White Rock Hills PHOTO: Wynne Benti

Corps camped during the hard years of the Great Depression to build the catch basin. It is a truly a beautiful spot above the White Rock Hills Continue up the trail passing a few more concrete foundations.

Slightly down off the trail, the spring is hidden behind non-native bamboo. As exotic and out of place as the bamboo seems, it's a beautiful setting. In the morning the White Rock Hills block the sun, shading the entire trail and spring on hot summer mornings. With an early start (as soon as the entrance gate opens, be on your way to the trailhead), this is quite a pleasant summer hike. Just be back at your car before the sun crawls over the crest of the hills.

North Peak Trail

Rating: Moderate
Recommended for: All well-conditioned dogs, any size
Round-trip mileage: 2.1 miles, 640' gain, 1-1.5 hours
K9 water: No water; 2-quarts minimum
Posted: Pets on leash. Clean up after your pet.
Ambience: Meandering trail through the high country of the La Madres
Best time to hike: Year-round. Snow and washouts possible.

We included this hike in this book, is because it is an official Red Rock NCA Trail. The North Peak/Bridge Mountain Trail is a wonderful, easily followed trail to the summit of North Peak, with awesome views of Bridge Mountain, across Red Rock to the Las Vegas strip.

Important Warning About Driving on Unmaintained Roads

The Rocky Gap 4x4 Road is an unmaintained/travel at your own risk road. The BLM posted a road closure sign at the Red Rock entrance station but the road is open at press time (this can change any time). We scouted Rocky Gap 4x4 Road from Willow Springs to Red Rock Summit/trailhead for North Peak in August, October and November of 2005 (the section needed to do this hike). It was rough in spots but driveable with a four-wheel drive.

DO NOT, we repeat, DO NOT attempt to approach Red Rock summit from the Pahrump-Lovell Canyon side via USFS 549. It is currently impassable to all four-wheel drives!

A Little Road History

The Rocky Gap 4x4 Road/USFS 549, was once known as the Old Road to Pahrump or the Potato Pass Road (Potato Pass is now called Red Rock Summit). It was the most direct route from Las Vegas to Pahrump, back when I-15 and SR-160 were non-existent. Back then, the state it was maintained and easily traveled in Model T's. Like many backcountry roads on public lands, Rocky Gap is currently unmaintained. We hope this status changes in the future because it is one of the great historic roads. Now, you drive it at your own risk. If you and your vehicle get stuck, you are responsible for getting out.

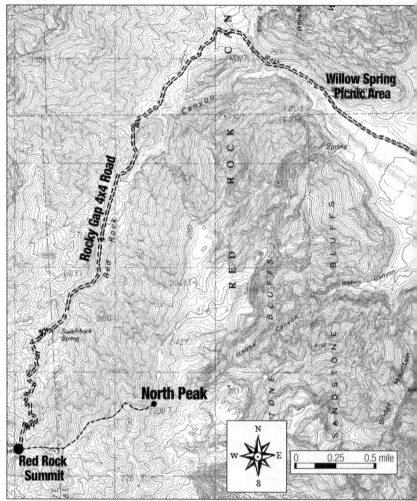

4x4 ONLY route from Willow Spring to Red Rock Summit PHOTO: Wynne Benti

Driving

Maps: Nevada Road & Recreation Atlas, AAA Las Vegas Vicinity Guide

From the Red Rock NCA entrance station, drive 7.3 miles to the paved White Rock Loop Road, turn right and set your odometer to zero. It is about 5.4 miles from here to Red Rock Summit. Drive 0.7 miles to the end of the paved road at Willow Springs Picnic Area, the beginning of the Rocky Gap 4x4 Road (drive at your own risk). Follow the road along the wash then across the wash. At 1.5 miles, note the trailhead for La Madre Springs on your right. Follow the road to Red Rock Summit at approximately 5.4 miles. The trailhead sign at Red Rock Summit is a welcome sight. Return the same way. ***Do not continue west toward Pahrump!***

If you get stuck, be prepared to walk back to Willow Springs. The only possible cell phone reception will be 911 from North Peak, and even then, reception is hit or miss.

View from the summit of North Peak
PHOTO: Wynne Benti

Hiking
Map: USGS La Madre Mountain (NV) 7.5-Minute (1:24,000 scale) Quad

From the signed trailhead just follow the well-worn trail up over the rise from the parking area. The trail meanders through a beautiful juniper forest. When the trail reaches the saddle with spectacular views across Bridge Mountain to Las Vegas, turn left and scramble the last couple hundred feet to the limestone summit. The views across the rugged limestone ridges of the La Madre Mountains behind you, and the Aztec sandstone of Red Rock to the Strip are quite spectacular.

The North Peak Trail is a beautiful, though waterless hike for dogs. Starting at about 6,604', it is usually ten to twenty degrees cooler than Red Rock in August. Directly below the summit in the red sandstone below, note the hidden forests and waterpockets within the sandstone folds around Bridge Mountain.

This is one of our favorite dog hikes in all of Red Rock. Hopefully the old historic road, now the Rocky Gap 4x4 Road, will be bladed once again in the future so that all visitors may enjoy this wonderful trail high above the Red Rock country.

WILLOW SPRINGS LOOP

Rating: Easy-moderate
Recommended for: Small, out-of-shape or older dogs
Round-trip mileage: 1.5 miles, 200' gain, 1 hour
K9 water: Seasonal water; 2-quart minimum
Posted: Pets on leash. Clean up after your pet.
Best time to hike: Year-round. Get an early morning start in summer.

Driving
Maps: Nevada Road & Recreation Atlas, AAA Las Vegas Vicinity Guide
From the Red Rock NCA entrance station, drive 7.3 miles to the paved White Rock Loop Road. Turn right and drive 0.7 miles to the end of the paved road at Willow Springs Picnic Area, also the beginning of the unmaintained Rocky Gap 4x4 Road to North Peak. since this is a loop trip, park either at the Willow Springs picnic area parking lot at the end of the road or at the Lost Springs parking area (see the Lost Creek Trail driving instructions).

Hiking
Maps: USGS La Madre Mountain (NV) 7.5-Minute (1:24,000 scale) Quad;
Green Trails Maps-Red Rock NCA #2474S
The trail starts at the Willow Springs picnic area just south of the restrooms. Walk south to the Lost Creek Trail parking area. At this parking area take the right fork (left goes across the wash to Lost Creek) north along the wash.

The petroglyphs PHOTO: Wynne Benti

PETROGLYPH TRAIL

Rating: Super easy
Recommended for: Small, out-of-shape or older dogs
Round-trip mileage: 0.2 miles, 20 minutes
K9 water: No water; 1-quart
Posted: Pets on leash. Clean up after your pet.
Best time to hike: Year-round. Get an early morning start in summer.

Driving
Maps: Nevada Road & Recreation Atlas, AAA Las Vegas Vicinity Guide
From the entrance station drive 7.3 miles to the paved White Rock Loop Road. Turn right and drive 0.7 miles to the end of the paved road at Willow Springs Picnic Area, also the beginning of the unmaintained Rocky Gap 4x4 Road. The sign for the Petroglyph Trail is just this side of the end of the road roundabout. Restrooms.

Hiking
Maps: USGS La Madre Mountain (NV) 7.5-Minute (1:24,000 scale) Quad;
Green Trails Maps-Red Rock NCA #2474S
This short trail crosses the pebbly-wash from the parking area to the cliffs on the other side. There is a wonderful view of petroglyphs well defined by thousands of years of desert varnish.

LOST CREEK TRAIL

Rating: Easy
Recommended for: Small, out-of-shape or older dogs
Round-trip mileage: 1.4 miles, 60' of gain, 1 hour
K9 water: Seasonal water at falls; 1-quart minimum
Posted: Pets on leash. Clean up after your pet.
Ambience: Nice hike to ephemeral Lost Creek waterfall
Best time to hike: Year-round. Get an early morning start in summer.

Driving

Maps: Nevada Road & Recreation Atlas, AAA Las Vegas Vicinity Guide

From the entrance station drive 7.3 miles to the paved White Rock Loop Road. Turn right and drive another 0.2 miles to the parking area on the left. Restrooms.

Hiking

Maps: USGS La Madre Mountain (NV) 7.5-Minute (1:24,000 scale) Quad;
Green Trails Maps-Red Rock NCA #2474S

Hike across the parking lot, and cross the pebble-filled wash to the wooden bridge on the other side. The bridge takes you to a

Bridge over riparian habitat PHOTO: Wynne Benti

lush foliage-filled desert paradise fed by natural springs and runoff from Lost Creek. The bridge is in place to protect the fragile riparian habitat from overuse. This area is being restored so please keep dogs on the bridge.

The trail meanders along toward the cliffs, passing by a nice shaded bench. The trail culminates at the falls, in a wisp of water dripping down from the high rocks above. The small waterfall flows much heavier in early spring after the winter snow melts in Red Rock's high country.

The kids are warmly dressed for their winter hike PHOTO: Megan Lawlor

CHILDREN'S DISCOVERY TRAIL

Rating: Moderate
Recommended for: Well-conditioned dogs, medium-sized and above
Round-trip mileage: 0.75 miles, 200' gain, 40 minutes
K9 water: No water; 1-quart minimum; seasonal water in wash
Posted: Pets on leash. Clean up after your pet.
Ambience: Look for migrating birds in a rather bleak setting
Best time to hike: November to April. Get an early morning start.

Driving

Maps: Nevada Road & Recreation Atlas, AAA Las Vegas Vicinity Guide

From the entrance station drive 7.3 miles to the paved White Rock Loop Road. Turn right and drive another 0.2 miles to the parking area on the left. Restrooms.

Hiking

Maps: USGS La Madre Mountain; Green Trails Maps-Red Rock NCA #2474S; well-marked easy to follow trail

We included this hike only because the signed trailhead starts at

Lost Creek and people might wonder why we had missed it. The entire trail follows the broad, dry bed of the wash. It's all rocks and large gravel, and doesn't make for easy dog walking, especially for little or older dogs. It is an easy-to-follow trail, but it's actually one of the least interesting trails in the park from a canine standpoint!

Children's Discovery Trail
PHOTO: Wynne Benti

Ice Box Canyon Trail

Rating: Moderate-strenuous
Recommended for: Well-conditioned dogs, medium-sized and above
Round-trip mileage: 2.8 miles, 560' gain, 2 hours
K9 water: No water; 2-quart minimum; seasonal waterpockets in wash
Posted: Pets on leash. Clean up after your pet.
Ambience: Rugged hike up narrow boulder-strewn canyon to seasonal waterfalls–lots of boulder-hopping
Best time to hike: November to April. Get an early morning start.

Driving
Maps: Nevada Road & Recreation Atlas, AAA Las Vegas Vicinity Guide
From the Red Rock NCA entrance station drive about 8.0 miles to the trailhead parking area. Restrooms.

Hiking
Maps: USGS La Madre Mountain (NV) 7.5-Minute (1:24,000 scale) Quad;
Green Trails Maps-Red Rock NCA #2474S
From the parking lot head west on the signed trail across a wash, up some stone stairs and onto the alluvial fan. Pass the intersection with north-south trending Dale's Trail. There are a myriad of paths that all head to the mouth of the canyon. At the very mouth of the canyon, two final paths drop down into the rugged boulder-filled desert wash.

Look back when you drop down into the wash and make a visual notation of the route back up on to the alluvial fan. It is rugged boulder-hopping up and down culminating in a small series of pools in winter, but dry in August, lest you catch them after an afternoon thunderstorm.

Ice Box Canyon Trails
Ice Box Canyon: 2.5 miles difficult
Lost Creek: 1.3 miles (via Dale's Trail, north) moderate
Dale's Trail intersection: 0.2 miles
Pine Cree: 2.2 miles (via Dale's Trail south) mod-strenuous

Listen to the birds at the mouth of Ice Box Canyon, one of the driest washes in Red Rock during the summer months. PHOTO: Wynne Benti

Pine Creek Canyon Trail

Rating: Moderate
Recommended for: All well-conditioned dogs, any size
Round-trip mileage: 2.9 miles, 100' gain, 1-3 hours
K9 water: Water in creek; 2-quart minimum
Posted: Pets on leash. Clean up after your pet.
Ambience: One of the prettiest canyon trails in all of Red Rock with ruins, pine trees, an old grape orchard and Mescalito!
Best time to hike: November to April. Get an early morning start.

Driving
Maps: Nevada Road & Recreation Atlas, AAA Las Vegas Vicinity Guide
From the entrance station drive about 8.0 miles to the trailhead parking area. Restrooms.

Hiking
Maps: USGS Blue Diamond (NV) 7.5-Minute (1:24,000 scale) Quad;
Green Trails Maps-Red Rock NCA #2474S
The trail drops down a short hill from the parking lot, then cross over a wash. Head west on the trail towards the cliffs. About 0.6 miles up the trail is a short interpretive loop off to the left, south, called the Fire Ecology Trail. The Dale's Trail fork comes in around 0.75 miles.

When we scouted this hike in August, a small portion of the Pine Creek Trail had just burned, the fire caused by a lightning strike. The smell of burnt flora still lingered. We had the good fortune of hiking right after a thunderstorm. From the trail, we listened to water cascading down the cliffs all around us!

At the loop junction, take the right loop, north, returning on the south side loop (passing the Arnight Trail fork and an old two track Jeep trail) through Horace Wilson's Thompson seedless grape orchard which has grown wild wrapping vines and leaves throughout the meadow and trees—it is a beautiful sight on a summer's evening after a thunderstorm. Cross over Pine Creek to the foundation of the Horace Wilson homestead (no relation to James Wilson) that sits at the head of the lush meadow.

Annie and Ginger on the way to Pine Creek PHOTO: Megan Lawlor

Horace Wilson's Thompson seedless grapes grow wild in Pine Creek.
The haunting silhouette of Mescalito is in the background. PHOTO: Wynne Benti

PINE CREEK CANYON TRAILS

Pine Creek Canyon	2.9 miles	moderate
Fire Ecology Trail	1.0 miles	easy
Ice Box Canyon	2.5 miles	difficult
Arnight Trail	1.1miles	

DALE'S TRAIL
ICE BOX TO PINE CREEK

Rating: Moderate
Recommended for: All well-conditioned dogs, any size
Round-trip mileage: 5.0 miles, 3 hours
K9 water: No water; 1-2 quart minimum
Posted: Pets on leash. Clean up after your pet.
Ambience: Meandering trail through manzanita, pinyon, ponderosa
Best time to hike: November to April. Get an early morning start.

Driving
Maps: Nevada Road & Recreation Atlas, AAA Las Vegas Vicinity Guide
From the Red Rock NCA entrance station drive about 8.0 miles to the Ice Box Trailhead parking area. Restrooms.

Hiking
Maps: USGS Blue Diamond (NV) 7.5-Minute (1:24,000 scale) Quad;
Green Trails Maps-Red Rock NCA #2474S
From the parking lot head west on the signed trail across a wash, up some stone stairs and onto the alluvial fan. At about 0.2 miles turn left (south) on the north-south trending Dale's Trail.

This scenic and colorful trail follows the escarpment along the base of Bridge and Rainbow Mountain. About five to ten minutes along the trail, cross a wash which may be flowing briskly in early Spring. Walk slightly right and around the tree in the middle of the wash. Catch the trail on the other side and ascend a hill, then up and down over the rolling landscape. There is a wooden bench on the top of the hill and to the west. Rest if you like and take in the views.

Notes
Red Rock Scenic Loop was completed in the 1970s. Before then, various dirt roads led in and out of the canyons and some only accessible by four-wheel drive. Dale's Trail is only about 10 year old and according to the BLM was named after a dedicated volunteer who worked on the trail.

The palette of colors along this scenic trail is striking. The deep red, rust, peach, and cream colors of the majestic sandstone cliffs

Ginger takes in the view on Dale's Trail PHOTO: Megan Lawlor

look as if a giant took one large sweep with a paintbrush and placed them there. Here and there, a towering pine stands out among the thick outcropping of manzanita bushes, and along the washes grow desert willows. Desert willows have pale pink, tiny orchid-shaped flowers and because they grow along washes, they are very useful for erosion control.

If you are lucky enough in the spring, you may see red bud trees blooming (they look like a really large bush). These trees are our very favorites because of their brightly colored magenta flowers. There is usually one in the wash by the trailhead. Also in the spring, wildflowers cover the orange desert sand in every imaginable color. All this color against the deep blue sky and you're heaven. About halfway down the trail is a glorious view of Mt. Wilson and Rainbow Mountain. On the return hike the sun illuminates Turtlehead Peak and Sandstone Quarry. We spotted bighorn sheep once along this trail scurrying up the steep slopes.

OAK CREEK TRAIL
TO OAK CREEK SPRING

Rating: Moderate
Recommended for: All well-conditioned dogs, any size
Round-trip mileage: 3.2 miles, 260' gain, 2 hours
K9 water: Water; 2-quarts minimum
Posted: Pets on leash. Clean up after your pet.
Ambience: Creek is hidden deep within thick vines
Best time to hike: November to April. Get an early morning start.

Driving
Maps: Nevada Road & Recreation Atlas, AAA Las Vegas Vicinity Guide
From the Red Rock entrance station drive about 11.8 miles on the one-way scenic drive and turn right (west) on gravel road. Drive another 0.6 miles to the Oak Creek Trailhead parking area. Restrooms.

Hiking
Maps: USGS Blue Diamond (NV) 7.5-Minute (1:24,000 scale) Quad;
Green Trails Maps-Red Rock NCA #2474S
From the parking area, head south on the Oak Creek Canyon Trail about 0.6 miles to North Oak Creek Trail. Turn right, west,

towards the cliffs. Near the mouth of the canyon, if you listen you can hear trickling water, almost year-round. In summer, parts of the creek are completely bone dry in places while in other spots water bubbles out into clear cool pools. Listen not only to the water, but the sound of song birds in the canyon.

Rosy smells the lush foliage and listens to the echoes of the canyon wrens
PHOTO: Wynne Benti

Arnight-Knoll-Oak Creek Trail Loop

Rating: Easy-moderate
Recommended for: All well-conditioned dogs, any size
Round-trip mileage: 3.5 miles, minimal gain, 1.5-2 hours
K9 water: No water on trail; 2-quarts minimum
Posted: Pets on leash. Clean up after your pet.
Ambience: Beautiful trail across the open desert just to touch the edge of two magnificent canyons
Best time to hike: November to April. Get an early morning start.

Driving

Maps: Nevada Road & Recreation Atlas, AAA Las Vegas Vicinity Guide

From Red Rock NCA entrance station, drive 11.8 miles to the signed dirt road to Oak Creek, turn right and drive 0.6 miles to the parking area. The signed Arnight Trail begins on the north side of the parking lot. Restrooms.

Hiking

Maps: USGS Blue Diamond (NV) 7.5-Minute (1:24,000 scale) Quad;
Green Trails Maps-Red Rock NCA #2474S

This is a beautiful loop trail that touches the mouths of two canyons: Pine Creek and Oak Creek. From north end of parking lot, take the signed, very well-worn Arnight Trail north to Pine Creek Canyon, staying left at all forks. The red trail crosses the rolling desert above Red Rock through a native garden of blue-green sage and yellow-colored cactus, yucca, juniper and a multitude of grasses. Just after sunset, in September, the Red Rock "alpenglow" intensifies the color of the desert flora, especially the yellow grasses. The trail crosses a wash of red and pink stones.

The burros often hang out along Pine Creek on summer evenings and can be heard braying down in the camouflaged cover of lower Pine Creek or be met along the trail. The beds they have made can be seen as you pass an area of flattened grasses. As Arnight Trail nears the southern walls of Pine Creek Canyon, a trail marker and junction with the Knoll Trail is reached. The right

Rosy on the Arnight Trail around sunset PHOTO: Wynne Benti

fork continues on to Pine Creek. Take the left fork, Knoll Trail, which begins to turn back south after getting just a little closer to the great walls before you. The Knoll Trail is not quite as well traveled as most of the other trails in this book, and though slightly overgrown, it is followed with relative ease. The trail crosses back down into the red wash over a series of steep, hand-hewn steps then across the undulating desert terrain to the north side of Oak Creek Canyon and the junction with the Oak Creek Trail. At dusk, it is a wonderland of small mammals and birds making their vocal calls to neighbors as they venture out into the early evening. Tiny bats whirl and gyrate just above the trail catching bugs. Turn left to the parking lot, which is in plain view, a very lovely and easy mile down the trail. Arrive at the opposite end of the parking lot at the New Oak Creek Trail system sign.

Oak Creek Canyon
From The South Oak Creek Trail

Rating: moderate
Recommended for: All well-conditioned dogs, any size
Round-trip mileage: 5.6 miles, 480' gain, 40' loss, 2-3 hours
K9 water: Seasonal water in creek; 2-quart minimum
Posted: Pets on leash. Clean up after your pet. No facilities.
Ambience: Across the desert plain into deep thickets to cool clear water
Best time to hike: November to April. Get an early morning start.

Driving
Maps: Nevada Road & Recreation Atlas, AAA Las Vegas Vicinity Guide
From the intersection of the 215-Western Beltway and 159/West Charleston Blvd., drive west on SR-159 approximately 5.2 miles to the entrance for the Red Rock Scenic Drive. Note your odometer. From the entrance gate continue on SR-159 approximately 3.7 miles to the signed Oak Creek trailhead. Park on the right. No facilities.

Hiking
Maps: USGS Blue Diamond (NV) 7.5-Minute (1:24,000 scale) Quad;
Green Trails Maps-Red Rock NCA #2474S
From the parking lot follow the very wide trail across a wash, then over rambling desert terrain—yucca, Joshua trees, cholla and wild grasses toward the high cliffs. SR-159 is in view most of the way. The trail climbs a short grade as it nears the cliffs, then drops down into red sandy, grass-covered terrain and a myriad of foot paths. The main trail stays south, closest to the cliffs, and continues into the canyon, but the creek and its water can be reached by one of many footpaths before the mouth of the canyon.

The key is picking the right path to the creek as some deadend in a mass of vines and trees. A secret path about two hundred feet above two large pine trees in the wash weaves in and out of dark cavelike thickets to the creek. Step lightly across vines to the creek bed. In summer, the creek is bone dry in places, while cold fresh water percolates out of the ground a few feet away. This is a great place to watch birds and listen to their music.

Ivy in Oak Creek PHOTO: Wynne Benti

FIRST CREEK CANYON TRAIL
TO FIRST CREEK SPRING

Rating: Moderate
Recommended for: All well-conditioned dogs, any size
Round-trip mileage: 3.4 miles round-trip, 280' gain, 1-2 hours
K9 water: Seasonal water in creek; 2-quart minimum
Posted: Pets on leash. Clean up after your pet. No facilities.
Ambience: Gentle trail across the red desert to a peaceful creek and canyon
Best time to hike: November to April.

Driving
Maps: Nevada Road & Recreation Atlas, AAA Las Vegas Vicinity Guide
From the intersection of the 215-Western Beltway and 159/West Charleston Blvd., drive west on SR-159 approximately 5.2 miles to the entrance for the Red Rock Scenic Drive. Note your odometer. From the entrance gate continue on SR-159 approximately 4.3 miles to the signed First Creek Trailhead, about 0.6 miles past the second or south Oak Creek parking area (marked by a no camping sign). No facilities.

Hiking
Maps: USGS Blue Diamond (NV) 7.5-Minute (1:24,000 scale) Quad;
Green Trails Maps-Red Rock NCA #2474S
From the parking lot follow the trail west across gentle rolling desert terrain—yucca, Joshua trees, cholla and wild grasses. The trail meanders through undulating grasslands to the creek. Look for the biggest pine tree near the canyon mouth. The creek can be easily accessed near the tree.

This area is a favorite grazing spot for burros. We've seen as many as two dozen burros at one time. Because people feed the burros, they have become habituated to human food and may come sprinting over to you. They may also be after your dog, thinking it a coyote. Like wild horses or range cattle, a burro too will kill a dog by kicking or stomping it to death.

This is a great summer walk in early evening, especially after a thunderstorm. The lighting as the western sun sets casts a reddish-golden glow across the desert.

BLACK VELVET LOOP

Rating: Easy-moderate
Recommended for: All well-conditioned dogs, any size
Round-trip mileage: 3.5 miles, minimal gain, 1.5 hours
K9 water: Seasonal water in Lower Mud Springs; 2-quart minimum
Posted: Pets on leash. Clean up after your pet. No facilities.
Ambience: Classic trail across varied desert terrain to a spring
Best time to hike: October to April. Get an early morning start.

Driving
Maps: Nevada Road & Recreation Atlas, AAA Las Vegas Vicinity Guide
From the intersection of SR-159 and SR-160, drive north on SR-160, 4.7 miles to a dirt road (#201) and turn right. Set your odometer to zero and drive as follows: at 1.4 miles stay right at a triangular inter- section; 2.0 miles left at fork; 2.5 miles left at T-fork. At 3.3 miles reach a parking area at the end of the road.

Hiking
Maps: USGS Blue Diamond (NV) 7.5-Minute (1:24,000 scale) Quad;
Green Trails Maps-Red Rock NCA #2474S
Walk west to the trailhead, marked at press time by a rustic, hand- written BLM sign. Follow the well-worn path west towards the canyon, staying left at the first fork (right goes into Black Velvet Canyon). Head southwest along the trail staying right at a restoration sign. There is quite a bit of cholla along the high part of this route. Follow the well-worn trail up and down through nature's desert. The trail passes to the right of "Luxor Rock" the unofficial name for a large pyramidal-shaped boulder. The trail turns south away from the cliffs, across the alluvial plain of the open desert approaching a large east-west trending wash. The trail turns east paralleling the wash for awhile, then turns south and crosses the wash to a T-fork on the other side. Turn left on the Black Velvet Trail (right is the Late Night Trail) which merges with a dirt road. Cross a second wash staying left at the fork in the wash. Reach a trail marker and turn left on the Outer Loop Trail. The road parallels the south side of the wash. Lower Mud Springs comes into view and flows all year long after heavy winters.

Lower Mud Springs on the PHOTO: Wynne Benti

Follow dirt road east to a trail marker for Inner/Outer Loop. Turn north on Outer Loop Trail and drop down into the wash and Lower Mud Springs. Stay on the trail as it meanders through the red sands of Mud Springs, an area currently closed for riparian habitat restoration. The temptation is great to walk the inviting spur washes off to the left back to the car. The trail winds somewhat circuitously through Mud Springs but takes you to the dirt road back to the parking lot. Turn left on the dirt road at the Black Velvet Trail sign, then head west back to the car.

WHEELER CAMP SPRING
TO LANDMINE LOOP TRAIL AND BACK

Rating: Easy
Recommended for: All well-conditioned dogs, any size
Round-trip mileage: 1.0 mile, 60' gain. 1 hour
K9 water: Water; 1-quart minimum
Posted: Pets on leash. Clean up after your pet. No facilities.
Ambience: Wash shaded by cottonwoods during the summer
Best time to hike: Year-round.

Driving
Maps: Nevada Road & Recreation Atlas, AAA Las Vegas Vicinity Guide
From the intersection of 160/159 take SR-159 drive 3.8 miles (just past the town of Blue Diamond) and turn left over a cattle guard into the signed parking lot for Wheeler Spring.
Alternate route:
From 215/159 West Charleston Blvd. take SR-159 west approximately 12.0 miles to the cattle guard and turn right (about 1.2 miles past the entrance to Old Nevada/Bonnie Springs). If you get to Blue Diamond, you've gone to far. No facilities.

Hiking
Maps: USGS Blue Diamond (NV) 7.5-Minute (1:24,000 scale) Quad;
Green Trails Maps-Red Rock NCA #2474S
Walk west through gates straight ahead to creek, and turn left toward Blue Diamond. Older dogs can meander in and out of the creek (toward Blue Diamond) to the fenced property line and back. During the summer, the main creek is generally dry, but there is a spring about an eighth of a mile down, on the west side of the wash.

At the gabions (stones encased in chicken wire for flood control, developed by the French) in the creek bed, turn west on any of the foot paths on the west side of the creek that head up to the small cliffs above to a trail that runs just above the wash. Continue south toward Blue Diamond. Pass through a little gate (please close), then turn right on the Landmine Loop Trail (not signed), a popular mountain bike trail. This trail turns you north back

Jeff and Ginger at Wheeler Camp PHOTO: Megan Lawlor

toward the high cliffs of Red Rock. About 0.5 mile up the trail, a natural fence of limestone rock crosses the trail. Just before this geological landmark, turn right (north) and drop down into the wash . Continue back to the parking lot which is in plain view.

Flash floods can occur any time. Check weather conditions prior to your hike. Do not hike or drive across any flooded path.

Notes

This is a beautiful spot with a long history. Travelers along the Old Spanish Trail stopped here to water their horses but it was reported that the water was so bitter, future parties chose to camp at springs (now Bonnie Springs) a few miles back. In 1871, the Wheeler Survey Party, under the supervision of George M. Wheeler camped here and watered their horses. Wheeler was charged with surveying and preparing maps on the U.S Territory south of the Central Pacific Railroad, to prepare reports on the Native American, select sites for future military installations, rail

Gate from Wheeler Camp to
Landmine Loop junction
PHOTO: Wynne Benti

and road route as well as the overall natural resources. United States. Army. Corps of Engineers. The following reports were prepared from this particular excursion: *Preliminary Report Concerning Explorations and Surveys Principally in Nevada and Arizona... Conducted under the Immediate Direction of 1st Lieut. George M. Wheeler, Corps of Engineers. 1871. F 841.A33. United States. Geographical Surveys West of the 100th Meridian. Annual Report upon Geographical and Geological Explorations and Surveys West of the One Hundredth Meridian in California, Nevada, Utah, Arizona, Colorado, New Mexico, Wyoming, and Montana by George M. Wheeler. 1874. 917.8 Un581a.*

The site was a popular party spot and was often littered with trash, broken glass and spent shotgun shells. The Red Rock Audobon Society spent many volunteer hours restoring this beautiful riparian habitat back to its natural state. It is a excellent birding location for native and migratory species. Bring your plastic bags to pick up after your dog.

Spring Mountain Ranch

History

What an interesting history this gem of the Nevada State Park system has. With its natural springs known to the local Paiute Indians and their ancestors for centuries, this area was first used by Europeans travelling through the Cottonwood Valley as an alternate route to the Old Spanish Trail circa 1834. Use of this route continued until the wagons were replaced by the railroad in 1905.

In 1840, after participating in raids on Mexican ranches in California, American frontiersman Bill Williams rested and watered his horses at this site. A trapper, horseman, and guide for wagon trains traveling from Fort Leavenworth, Kansas to Santa Fe, Williams also guided for John C. Fremont. Though Williams was killed by Indians in 1849, this stopover and watering hole was known as the old Bill Williams Ranch for almost thirty years after his death.

Located on the back of the property is a sandstone cabin and blacksmith shop that were built in 1864 by grain merchants from the now defunct mining town of Ivanpah. These two buildings

Stand of native Arizona ash, *Fraxinus velutina*   PHOTO: Wynne Benti

are the second oldest in Las Vegas and the only completely intact buildings from that era in all of Southern Nevada.

In 1876, U.S. Army Sergeant James Wilson (who was stationed at Fort Mohave and for whom Wilson Peak is named) and his partner George Anderson filed a deed on the land and ranched cattle. They planted fruit trees, harvested grain and vegetables which were sold to miners in the districts of Ivanpah, Potosi, and El Dorado Canyon along Lake Mojave.

When the ranch fell on hard times, it was purchased by a well-known furrier named Willard George who placed a covenant on the deed allowing Wilson's sons Tweed and Jim Jr. to live there for the rest of their lives. The ranch was later owned by early radio personality Chet Lauck, German actress and millionairess Vera Krupp, millionaire Howard Hughes, and Las Vegas car dealer Fletcher Jones. Jones sold the ranch to the state of Nevada in 1974 after his attempts to develop it failed.

In addition to several equestrian trails on the flats, there are two hiking trails, Ash Grove Nature Trail and the Overlook Trail.

Inquisitive burro at a natural spring at Ash Grove   PHOTO: Wynne Benti

OVERLOOK TRAIL
SPRING MOUNTAIN RANCH STATE PARK

Rating: Moderate
Recommended for: Well-conditioned dogs, any size
Round-trip mileage: 0.6 mile, 100' gain, 30 minutes
K9 water: No water; 1-quart minimum
Posted: Pets on leash. Clean up after your pet.
Ambience: Short walk to a beautiful view
Best time to hike: Year-round. Get an early morning start in summer.

Driving
Maps: Nevada Road & Recreation Atlas, AAA Las Vegas Vicinity Guide
Same as Ash Grove Nature Trail
Hiking
Maps: USGS Blue Diamond (NV) 7.5-Minute (1:24,000 scale) Quad;
Green Trails Maps-Red Rock NCA #2474S
The signed trail, one of the oldest original trails in this area, is
located on the west side of the parking lot (on your right) before

you start up to the ranch
house. It is a short, some
what steep little hike
through desert scrub to a
nice overlook of the state
park, the sandstone cliffs
and north into Red Rock.

The creek through Ash Grove in August   PHOTO: Wynne Benti

Ash Grove Nature Trail
Spring Mountain Ranch State Park

Rating: Easy
Recommended for: All well-conditioned dogs, any size
Round-trip mileage: 0.8 mile, minimal gain, 45 minutes-1 hour
K9 water: Ephemeral creek on the walk; 1-quart minimum
Posted: Pets on leash. Clean up after your pet.
Ambience: A pleasant interpretive walk through the only native Arizona Ash grove in Red Rock. Shaded most of the way. Disabled access on gravel loop trail before the main loop.
Best time to hike: November to April.

Driving
Maps: Nevada Road & Recreation Atlas, AAA Las Vegas Vicinity Guide
From the intersection of the 215-Western Beltway and 159/West Charleston Blvd., drive west on SR-159 approximately 10.0 miles to the ranch entrance and turn right. Follow signs to the parking area. Restrooms. Park hours: 8am-5pm, daily.

Hiking
Maps: USGS Blue Diamond (NV) 7.5-Minute (1:24,000 scale) Quad;
Green Trails Maps-Red Rock NCA #2474S
Just above the parking lot is a shaded picnic area with a nice grassy lawn for old dogs to wander. From the parking lot, walk the white rail fence to the ranch house. As you face the ranch house, the signed trail is off to the left. Most folks have turned hard right past the sign, down a short hill along the fence or walk straight along the gravel trail to the main loop. Follow either trail and the interpretive signs through a sandy flat where burros roll in the sand to wash.

Cross a desert creek to the native Arizona ash grove, a natural spring frequented by desert wildlife, a tree pecked by woodpeckers, and great views of the great sandstone cliffs of Red Rock. If you bring your dog and want to see the ranch, plan for winter so you can leave your dog in the car for the half-hour tour.

Early morning light on Blue Diamond Wash   PHOTO: Wynne Benti

BLUE DIAMOND WASH
BLUE DIAMOND

Rating: Super easy
Recommended for: Small, out-of-shape or older dogs
Round-trip mileage: 0.6 mile, 30 minutes
K9 water: Seasonal water; 1-quart minimum
Best time to hike: Year-round.

Driving
Maps: Nevada Road & Recreation Atlas, AAA Las Vegas Vicinity Guide
From the intersection of the 215-Western Beltway and 159/West
Charleston Blvd., drive west on 159 about 13.3 miles to Arroyo Street,
the second exit for Blue Diamond. Continue about 0.5 mile past
Arroyo and make a right on a gravel road. Park, careful not to block
the road and walk down to the wash.

Hiking
Maps: USGS Blue Diamond (NV) 7.5-Minute (1:24,000 scale) Quad;
Green Trails Maps-Red Rock NCA #2474S

Along the Blue Diamond Wash   PHOTO: Wynne Benti

Pretty much anything goes here. We usually walk down to the wash and follow it left, south as far as we can walk, past the fenced ponds. The Blue Diamond mine is often operating in the hills above and to the east of the wash, with great chimneys of steam billowing out into the skyline. On Sundays, it's usually pretty quiet. Often a desert breeze makes for a beautiful walk in this classic wash. When the creek is dry, we'll park just off 159 on Arroyo Street in Blue Diamond and walk the dirt road between the highway and the wash all the way to the fenced ponds.

LAKE MEAD

WEATHER

Winter through early spring are the best times to hike Lake Mead, Lake Mojave or any stretch of the Colorado River in the Mojave Desert with your canine friend. Winters are wonderfully mild with average daytime temperatures in the 60s to 70s. In the summer, triple digits temps are the norm and not for dogs! Shade is at a premium and hot ground surfaces between car and trail will burn paws. *Do not* hike this area with dogs during the summer months.

LOW WATER LEVELS

It wasn't that long ago that you could see water in Echo Wash from Northshore Scenic Drive. At press time, the water level at Lake Mead National Recreation Area was at its lowest recorded level in forty years, closing a few of the boat launches. As a result there are not as many cars or people. Government Wash and Las Vegas Wash boat launches are virtual ghost towns. It's eerie to see the water line so far away from the end of the concrete ramp. In a way it's a boon to hikers who want more of a wilderness experience.

HISTORY

Named after Dr. Elwood Mead, U.S. Bureau of Reclamation Commissioner from 1924 to 1936, Lake Mead is the largest man-made reservoir in the United States. It's creation was born from the com-

19th century Paiute petroglyph of John Wesley Powell   PHOTO: Florine Lawlor

pletion of Hoover Dam in 1935. The project's "official" start date was September 17, 1930, the day that Secretary of the Interior Ray Lyman Wilbur presided over the Silver Spur Ceremony dedication of Union Pacific Railroad's new branch line from Las Vegas to the site of Boulder City. The Great Depression had started under Herbert Hoover's presidency. It was a terrible time to name the dam after the president, since most Americans blamed him for the country's financial demise. The dam's name changed several times from Hoover Dam to Boulder Dam, then back to Hoover Dam. It is estimated that more than 20,000 people made jobless by the 1929 stock market crash and subsequent depression, came to Southern Nevada to work on the construction of the dam.

Human habitation of Southern Nevada dates as far back to 13,000 B.C. with much of it located along the fertile river plains of the Colorado and its neighboring rivers. From 2000 BC to about 300 BC, the Gypsum-period people inhabited the area. The Moapa and Muddy River phases followed from about 700 AD to 1150 AD, the era of Lost City or Pueblo de Grande Nevada. Just across the river from the old Mormon townsite of St. Thomas, Pueblo de Grande Nevada was the largest single prehistoric occupation in the state.

The Anasazi (Navajo for "enemy ancestors" in reference to the prehistoric predecessors of the Hopi Indians) or Ancestral Puebloan inhabited the site later, building on top of earlier structures. Southern Paiute followed the Anasazi by several centuries. The Anasazi harvested salt on the lake which they traded to other tribes. Their salt mines are located near Overton Beach and are visible when the water levels are low in the lake.

When the first Mormons came into the area, they established good relations with the Paiutes. The Mormons did not tolerate slavery, and until then, most of the Paiute nation in Southern Nevada had been decimated by the slave trade along the Old Spanish Trail. Eventually, as the Mormon settlers moved into the lush river valley above what was once the Lost City, the Paiutes were outnumbered and eventually died or moved out.

The first Europeans to reach the Colorado River were the Spaniards, sent west to claim the world and its riches for the Spanish monarchy and the Catholic church which had moved from Rome to Spain. In 1539, Francisco de Ulloa discovered the Colorado heading north on an expedition from the Gulf of California. A year later, Hernando de Alarcon set sail upriver from the Gulf, while Garcia Lopez de Cardenas of Coronado discovered the Grand Canyon.

While the American colonials fought the British for freedom along the Atlantic coast in 1776, Fathers Silvestre Velez de Escalante and Francisco Atanasio Dominguez crossed the Colorado at Glen Canyon. Later that year, Father Francisco Garces christened the river "Colorado," Spanish for red mud.

Mountain man Jim Bridger was the first European to set foot in this area describing it as barren and terrible. In 1857, Lieutenant Joseph C. Ives with the Corps of Topographical Engineers traveled upriver on the Colorado from the Gulf of California, reaching the confluence of the Colorado and Las Vegas Wash in 1858. Major John Wesley Powell made the first trip on the Colorado River in 1869. Powell ended his trip just upriver from Echo Wash and was taken by wagon to the town of St. Thomas, later abandoned and submerged in 1938 by the waters of the newly formed Lake Mead. Author Megan Lawlor's mother-in-law, Florine Lawlor, visited St. Thomas before it was vanished beneath Lake Mead's waters. As of press time, St. Thomas had resurfaced, and is now one of the hikes in this book.

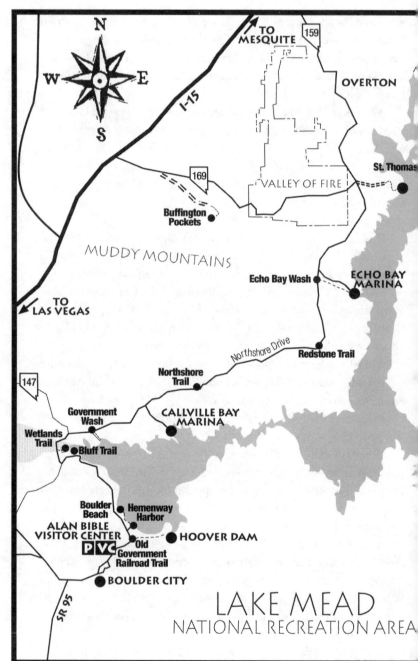

Mesa House reconstruction at Lost City Museum. PHOTO: Leslie Payne

Great Places to Visit

Editor's note: Sorry! Dogs aren't allowed in the museums.

Alan Bible Visitor Center

One of our favorite places to stop, the Alan Bible Visitor Center with its staff, volunteers and bookstore, is a wealth of information on the Lake Mead Area. It's located at the Boulder City entrance to Lake Mead just before the trailhead for the historic Old Government Railroad Trail.

Boulder City/Hoover Dam Museum

The Boulder City/Hoover Dam Museum, located in Boulder City, has an extensive collection of artifacts, oral histories and interpretive exhibits all pertaining to the building of the dam.

Lost City Museum

The Lost City Museum located in Overton tells the story of the Pueblo Grande de Nevada through interpretive exhibits and artifacts.

OLD GOVERNMENT RAILROAD TRAIL

Rating: Moderate
Recommended for: Well-conditioned dogs, any size
Round-trip mileage: 5.4 miles, minimal gain, 2 hours
K9 water: No water; 2-quart minimum
Posted: Pets on leash. Clean up after your pet.
Ambience: Historic walk along the old railroad grade built to construct what was then the world's largest dam
Best time to hike: November to April.
Early morning or late afternoon start any other time of the year.

Driving
Maps: Nevada Road & Recreation Atlas, AAA Las Vegas Vicinity Guide
From the junction of I-15 and US-95 take US-95/US-93/I-515 S south to Boulder City. Turn left on Buchanan Blvd./US 93. Set odometer to zero. Drive 3.7 miles to Lake Mead National Recreation Area/Alan Bible Visitor Center entrance and turn left, north. At 4.0 miles pass the Visitor Center entrance. At 4.2 miles turn right into the parking lot for the Historic Railroad Trail.

Hiking
The trail starts to the right of the interpretive sign, though a signed spur starts at the east end of the parking lot as well. Follow the well-worn foot path to the main trail, the old train grade, which heads east, paralleling US-93. Pass a spur trail to the casino (0.3 miles) up on US-93. Pass through two large gates to the entrance of the canyon. The grade follows the curve of the cliffs high above Lake Mead and Hemenway Marina. Follow the gentle grade through several tunnels to a fence along the trail just shy of Hoover Dam. Return the same way.

Notes
It was the 1931 christening of the historic railroad bed along this trail during the Silver Spur Ceremony that initiated the official start date of construction on Hoover Dam.

The trail follows the narrow gauge railroad bed used to haul freight during the construction of Hoover Dam in the 1930s. The train

Tunnels on the historic Old Government Railroad Trail PHOTO: Wynne Benti

operated twenty-four hours a day, seven days a week at the height of construction. The last train made its final trip in 1961. We have seen several bighorn sheep on the cliffs above the trail, near the trail's end on the Hoover Dam side.

Hemenway Harbor to Boulder Beach

Rating: Moderate
Recommended for: Well-conditioned dogs, any size
Round-trip mileage: 3.0 miles, minimal gain, 1.5 hours
K9 water: Water in lake; 2-quart minimum
Posted: Pets on leash. Clean up after your pet.
Ambience: Walk along the edge of Lake Mead to long sandy beach
Best time to hike: November to April.

Driving

Maps: Nevada Road & Recreation Atlas, AAA Las Vegas Vicinity Guide
From the junction of I-15 and US-95, take US-95/US-93/I-515 south to Boulder City. Turn left at Buchanan Blvd. Set odometer to zero. At 3.7 miles turn left at signed Lake Mead NRA-Alan Bible Visitor Center (Lakeshore Drive). At 4.8 miles pass through LMNRA entrance station. At 5.0 miles turn right to Las Vegas Boat Marina. At 5.9 miles turn left at Hemenway Boat Harbor, then at 6.0 miles turn right to Hemenway Fishing Point. Pass restrooms at 6.3 miles. Park.

Hiking

This walk is pretty straight forward—walk along the cove just above the water. Then follow the water's edge to Boulder Beach, the large sandy beach north of you. About 1.5 miles up the beach and to the left is the Boulder Beach Ranger Station and a shaded picnic area.

Of course, if you don't feel like walking very far, drive to the Boulder Beach Ranger Station parking area and hike down to the water from there. This is suitable for all dogs.

Notes

We love to take our dogs to Boulder Beach and have been doing it for more than twenty years. It's a wide sandy beach just below the Boulder Beach Ranger Station, where dogs are welcome on leash. Most of the time we go, we have the beach to ourselves.

BLUFF TRAIL
FROM LAS VEGAS CAMPGROUND

Rating: Easy
Recommended for: Well-conditioned dogs, any size
Round-trip mileage: 2.0 miles, minimal gain, 1 hour
K9 water: No water; 1 quart minimum
Posted: Pets on leash. Clean up after your pet.
Ambience: Walk along the edge of Lake Mead to long sandy beach
Best time to hike: October to April.

w of Lake Mead from Bluff Trail PHOTO: Wynne Benti

Driving

Maps: Nevada Road & Recreation Atlas, AAA Las Vegas Vicinity Guide

From the junction of I-15 and US-95 take US-95/US-93/I-515 south to Boulder City. Set your odometer to zero and turn left at Buchanan Blvd. At 3.7 miles turn left at signed Lake Mead NRA-Alan Bible Visitor Center entrance. Drive approximately 11.2 miles to Las Vegas Bay and turn right. At 11.3 miles, turn left at Las Vegas Bay Campground sign. At about 12.0 miles park in the small parking area just inside the entrance at information kiosk on right. Walk toward the first restroom and take the left fork, past the "DO NOT ENTER" sign marking a one-way road. Trail starts to the right of campground space #74.

Alternate driving route

From Las Vegas, take Hwy. 95 south to Lake Mead Parkway and exit. Turn left and follow Lake Mead Parkway, past Lake Las Vegas to the

The Bluff Trail overlooks the Las Vegas Wash with spectacular sightings of wildlife high above the sound of rapids PHOTO: Wynne Benti

Lake Mead National Recreation Area entrance station. From the entrance station, drive 0.3 miles and bear right to Lakeshore Scenic Drive. Drive 1.7 miles to Las Vegas Bay and turn left.

Hiking

Follow the well-worn trail from the campground across the top of the plateau. Below the trail is a beautiful creek, the primary drainage into Lake Mead from the Las Vegas Valley. Its rapids can be heard all along the first portion of the trail. A spectacular variety of birds can be seen including blue herons and egrets. The trail turns away from the river canyon, crossing the open desert and eventually ends at a promontory overlooking Lake Mead, Lake Las Vegas and Lakeshore Drive. Return by the same route.

Notes

The National Park Service pamphlet mistakenly notes the trail mileage as four miles round-trip. This trail is an easy two miles round-trip.

Wetlands Trail

Rating: Easy
Recommended for: All dogs
Round-trip mileage: 1.0 mile, 80' loss, minimal gain, 1 hour
K9 water: No water; 1 quart minimum
Posted: Pets on leash. Clean up after your pet.
Ambience: Such a beautiful spot! It's hard to imagine that the entire Vegas Valley runoff drains here!
Best time to hike: October to April.

Driving

Maps: Nevada Road & Recreation Atlas, AAA Las Vegas Vicinity Guide

From the junction of I-15 and US-95, take US-95/US-93/I-515 south to Boulder City. Set your odometer to zero and turn left at Buchanan Blvd. At 3.7 miles turn left at signed Lake Mead NRA-Alan Bible Visitor Center entrance. Drive approximately 12.9 miles to the Northshore Scenic Drive (Callville-Overton) and turn right. Drive 1.0 mile to a parking area on the right side of the road. Restroom.

Alternate driving route

From Las Vegas, take US-95 south to Lake Mead Parkway and exit. Turn left and take Lake Mead Parkway past Lake Las Vegas to the Lake Mead National Recreation Area entrance station. From the entrance station, drive 0.3 miles. Turn left on the Northshore Scenic Drive (Callville-Overton). At 1.0 mile turn right into a parking area.

Hiking

The trail starts between two posts. Follow it down a short steep ridge, where the trail forks. The fork straight ahead goes to an overlook. The right trail goes down to the water, but not without some scrambling over a ledge to the sand. This is the trail to take to get a closer view of the water and to walk along its edge as far as you can. The left trail bypasses the water altogether and heads back up to the parking lot.

Notes

This riparian habitat is rich with wildlife and is a birder's paradise with its vast assortment of native and migratory birds which change depending on the time of year. The opportunities for viewing wildlife

Wetlands Trail PHOTO: Wynne Benti

are spectacular. We saw two great blue herons and several great American egrets.

This creek with its steep-walled canyon setting, is one of the prettiest locations at Lake Mead. According to a Park Service volunteer at the campground, the creek apparently serves as the primary drainage for the entire Las Vegas Valley, resulting in a high bacteria count. Wouldn't recommend letting your dog swim in it. It's true it's going right into Lake Mead, the drinking water reservoir for millions of people downstream. By the time it reaches the water glass, it has been chemically treated again. Closest canine access to the lake is at Las Vegas Bay at the bottom of the boat launch (closed due to low water as press time) just a short two mile drive back on Lakeshore Scenic Drive.

Great views of the Bowl of Fire from the meandering Northshore Trail PHOTO: Wynne Benti

NORTHSHORE TRAIL

Rating: Moderate
Recommended for: All dogs
Round-trip mileage: 2.0 mile, 100' loss, minimal gain, 1 hour
K9 water: No water; 1 quart minimum
Posted: Pets on leash. Clean up after your pet.
Ambience: Vermillion cliffs in the heart of the Bowl of Fire
Best time to hike: October to April. Get an early morning start.

Driving

Maps: Nevada Road & Recreation Atlas, AAA Las Vegas Vicinity Guide

From the junction of I-15 and US-95, take US-95/US-93/I-515 south and exit at Lake Mead Parkway. Turn left, northeast. Follow Lake Mead Parkway, past Lake Las Vegas, to the Lake Mead National Recreation Area entrance station. From the entrance, drive 0.3 miles. Turn left on the Northshore Scenic Drive (Callville-Overton). At 19.0 miles turn left into the parking area.

Hiking

Walk signed the trail from the parking lot up the steep, short rise where the Bowl of Fire can be seen on the left. Take the right fork and continue on the trail, staying right at all forks until the trail appears to deadend at an outcropping of volcanic rock at the last fork. From here a left fork takes off to the heart of the Bowl of Fire, a spectacular of ancient Aztec sandstone. Thrust faults, where Bonanza King formation meets the vermillion-colored Aztec sandstone can be seen.

Government Wash

Rating: Moderate cross-country
Recommended for: Well-conditioned dogs, any size
Round-trip mileage: 3.0 mile, minimal gain, 1.5 hours
K9 water: Water at lake; 2-quarts minimum
Posted: Pets on leash. Clean up after your pet.
Ambience: Lovely walk down a wide desert wash
Best time to hike: October to April. Do not hike during thunderstorms, heavy water runoff or after heavy rains (soft, slick mud)

Driving
Maps: Nevada Road & Recreation Atlas, AAA Las Vegas Vicinity Guide
From the junction of I-15 and US-95, take US-95/US-93/I-515 south to Lake Mead Parkway and exit. Turn left, northeast, and follow Lake Mead Parkway, past Lake Las Vegas to the Lake Mead National Recreation Area entrance station. From the entrance station drive 0.3 miles to Northshore Scenic Drive and turn left towards Callville-Overton. Drive approximately 5.4 miles to Government Wash. Just on the other side of the wash at 5.6 miles is a gated service road. Two or three cars can park here, careful not to block the gate. Another option is to drive a few hundred feet up the road past the gate and park in the pullout just up Northshore Scenic Drive.

Hiking
From the locked gate follow the dirt track down to the telephone poles, then south down the wash, walking along the shaded east side. Take in the surroundings. On the left, low cliffs give way to a rolling landscape with desert pavement that has not been disturbed by water for some time. About twenty minutes into the hike, the telephone poles and a pipeline leave the wash. Walking becomes easier in the center channel.

The road to the boat launch runs above the wash but is only visible in a few places. Government Cove comes into view. Closer to the mouth of the wash, the tamarisks and Russian thistle become thick and impassable. Look over to the right for a whitish rock outcropping topped by tufa. Scramble out of the wash to the right of this rock,

Government Wash PHOTO: Wynne Benti

across what were once freshwater clam beds, to the boat launch. At the top of the launch is a restroom and emergency phone. Turn left toward the water and walk to the end of the launch to a dirt road. Follow the dirt road a few hundred feet to the water's edge. At press time, the cove was easily accessed at this point. Return the same way.

Notes

This is a wide, beautiful wash. The closing of the boat ramp has contributed to a quieter hiking experience since there aren't as many people.

Before hiking, check the weather for rain in the general vicinity. Government Wash is one of the gentlest in Lake Mead with plenty of flash flood escape routes to high ground in the rare event that there is such an occurrence. Washes generally drain several square miles of desert terrain, with some washes being more prone to severe flash-flooding than others. It doesn't necessarily need to rain directly over your location in the wash to cause unexpected heavy run-off or a flash flood. Be aware of your surroundings and note the landscape around you in case you have to make a quick climb to higher ground.

Leave wash to right of this rock outcropping we call Hoodoo Hill
PHOTO: Wynne Benti

By observing the ground in the wash, one can tell by the cut of the soil where the flow of water is most likely to be the heaviest. Soil covered with desert pavement (a blanket of fine small stones). If planning a hike after a storm, wait a few days for the ground to dry out as it tends to get really soft especially below the boat launch.

Redstone Trail

Rating: Super-easy
Recommended for: All dogs
Round-trip mileage: 0.5 miles, 30 minutes
K9 water: No water; 1 quart minimum
Posted: Pets on leash. Clean up after your pet.
Ambience: Walk among the petrified remains of great sand dunes
Best time to hike: October to April.

Driving

Maps: Nevada Road & Recreation Atlas, AAA Las Vegas Vicinity Guide

From the junction of I-15 and US-95, take US-95/US-93/I-515 south to Lake Mead Parkway and exit. Turn left, northeast, and follow Lake Mead Parkway, past Lake Las Vegas to the Lake Mead National Recreation Area entrance station. From the entrance station drive 0.3

Along the Redstone Trail PHOTO: Wynne Benti

miles to Northshore Scenic Drive and turn left to Callville-Overton. Drive approximately 13.4 miles to the Redstone picnic area and turn right into parking lot.

Hiking

From the parking lot follow the trail as meanders around and through the bright red Aztec sandstone. These are the petrified remains of great sand dunes that once covered most of the southwest during the time of dinosaurs.

Along the Redstone Trail PHOTOS: Wynne Benti

Echo Wash

Rating: Strenuous as a round-trip walk
Moderately strenuous as a one-way walk to the Echo Bay campground
Recommended for: Well-conditioned dogs, medium-sized and above
Round-trip mileage: 7.0 miles, minimal gain
K9 water: No water; 3-quart minimum
Posted: Pets on leash. Clean up after your pet.
Ambience: Walk down large wash
Best time to hike: November to March. Get a very early morning start!

Driving

Maps: Nevada Road & Recreation Atlas, AAA Las Vegas Vicinity Guide

From the junction of I-15 and US-95, take US-95/US-93/I-515 south to Lake Mead Parkway and exit. Turn left, northeast, and follow Lake Mead Parkway, past Lake Las Vegas to the Lake Mead National Recreation Area entrance station. From the entrance station drive 0.3 miles to Northshore Scenic Drive and turn left towards Callville-Overton. Drive approximately 19.8 miles to the signed Echo Wash dirt road on the west side of the highway, Turn left and park anywhere off the highway.

Alternate driving route

From the junction of Hwy. 95 and I-15, head north on I-15 about 32 miles to the Valley of Fire State Park-Exit 75. From the exit, drive east about 20.2 miles to the Valley of Fire west entrance fee station. Set your odometer to zero and drive as follows:

0.0	West entrance fee station
8.0	Junction with Northshore Drive. Turn right, south.
10.6	Echo Bay Marina
12.7	Echo Wash

Turn right on signed Echo Wash dirt road on the west side of Northshore Drive. Park anywhere off the highway. The wash is very sandy and is four-wheel drive only. Do not drive it without at least two four-vehicles in the party equipped with shovels and boards.

Looking down Echo Wash PHOTO: Wynne Benti

Car Shuttle Driving Instructions

From Northshore Drive, turn east on the road to Echo Bay Marina. Drive 4.4 miles to the second campground and turn right, then right again to enter the campground's one-way loop drive (stay right at second internal loop). It's about 0.3 miles to the end of the campground road and a parking area at a locked gate (restrooms). Note the gateway in the fence on the wash side. This will be the way you'll come out to your car. Take a look at the other notable landmarks, primarily the palm trees. Most hikers will be quite happy when those palm trees come into view as they come down the wash.

Hiking

Depending on your mood and how much exercise you want to get, Echo Wash can be done either as a one way car shuttle (you need two cars) or a round-trip. From the parking area on the west side of Northshore Drive, follow the wash as it loops around back under Northshore Drive and then hike directly east. If you are planning to make a round-trip hike, remember your landmarks for the return to make sure you end up in the correct wash. It's not too hard to get lost as you'll eventually hit the road on the way back.

Sunken boat along the trail back to the campground   PHOTO: Wynne Benti

Buffalo Washington Park   PHOTO: Wynne Benti

HISTORIC ST. THOMAS SITE
1865-1938 LOOP TRAIL

Rating: Easy
Recommended for: All dogs
Round-trip mileage: 2.5 miles, minimal gain and loss, 1.5 hours
K9 water: No water; 2-quarts minimum
Posted: Pets on leash. Clean up after your pet.
Ambience: Walk to ruins of town abandoned to make way for Lake Mead
Best time to hike: October to April. Do not hike after heavy rains (soft, slick mud)

Driving

Maps: Nevada Road & Recreation Atlas, AAA Las Vegas Vicinity Guide

From the junction of I-15 and US-95, take US-95/US-93/I-515 south to

sy gets ready for the St. Thomas Loop Trail
PHOTO: Wynne Benti

Lake Mead Parkway and exit. Turn left, northeast, and follow Lake Mead Parkway, past Lake Las Vegas to the Lake Mead National Recreation Area entrance station. From the entrance station drive 0.3 miles to Northshore Scenic Drive and turn left towards Callville-Overton. Drive about 45.2 miles to the intersection of Valley of Fire State Park Road-169 and the St. Thomas Road-109 (1.0 mile past the Overton Beach exit). Turn right, east, on St. Thomas Road, good dirt, passable to all two wheel-drive vehicles (barring any unfore-

seen washouts). Drive 3.3 miles to the parking area. There are no facilities. Pack out all garbage. Metal detectors are prohibited.

Alternate driving route

From the junction of US-95 and I-15, head north on I-15 about 32.0 miles to the Valley of Fire State Park-Exit 75 and exit. Drive east about

Old foundation at St. Thomas PHOTO: Wynne Benti

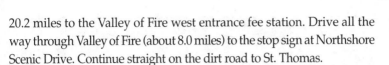
20.2 miles to the Valley of Fire west entrance fee station. Drive all the way through Valley of Fire (about 8.0 miles) to the stop sign at Northshore Scenic Drive. Continue straight on the dirt road to St. Thomas.

Hiking

Standing at the trailhead on the east side of the parking lot, ruins (pictured left) of the old townsite are visible to the south across the tamarisk-filled flats. Across the lake and to the north about a mile, beneath the bluffs, was the location of the largest occupied prehistoric site in Nevada, known as the Lost City, Pueblo Grande de Nevada.

Intact wood framing in the windows
PHOTO: Wynne Benti

This site was occupied first by Ancestral Puebloan, the Basketmakers, before 500 A.D. They first built pit houses, then houses over houses, sometimes two and three stories. They farmed on the fertile river plains of the Muddy River and mined salt at a large deposit south of Overton Beach, which they traded to other tribes. By 1100A.D., Pueblo Grande de Nevada, like so many other sites of that era, was abandoned.

From the parking area follow the well-marked trail down the embankment to the river flood plain now filled with the non-native tamarisk from India, introduced by the Army Corps of the Engineers in the early 20th century for erosion control. Just follow the signed trail as it turns south toward Overton Beach. Several spur trails disappear into the tamarisk, most of them made by curious visitors before the National Park Service cut the official trail. The easiest walking is on the wider, main trail. Staying right at all forks, the trail crosses over the largest ruins.

As the trail approaches town, the drowned, blackened corpses of dead trees become apparent through the tamarisk, even the remnants of what appears to be a small fruit orchard. Scattered among the broken shells of freshwater clams are pieces of lavender and green glass,

ABOVE: The National Park Service has their work cut out for them, clearing tamarisk along the trail to historic St. Thomas PHOTO: Wynne Benti
BELOW: Abandoned cars near the townsite of St. Thomas. Photograph from the collection of the James R. Dickinson Library, University of Nevada, Las Vegas

fragments of china cups and plates. Wood framing is still intact within the windows of one foundation, while the blackened branches of dead trees, shadowy apparitions, clutch the bleached concrete bones

of other ruins. Follow the trail through town center and back to the parking area.

Notes

With its fertile river bottom soil and plentiful water, St. Thomas and the surrounding area has had a long history of human habitation. The Southern Paiute had lived and farmed in this location for several centuries. By the mid-19th century, Mormon settlers arrived, and eventually so many came into the area, that the Paiutes literally died out by the early 20th century. In 1869, when John Wesley Powell's first exploratory trip down the Colorado River ended several miles upstream at a small Mormon settlement along the Colorado River, he was taken by wagon to St. Thomas. Las Vegas Review Journal columnist and third generation Las Vegas native, Florine Lawlor, visited St. Thomas at age 12 before it was submerged by waters from Lake Mead in 1938.

VALLEY OF FIRE

GEOLOGY

On the periphery of the Great Basin and Range and the Colorado Plateau, is the Valley of Fire. Its intense vermillion-colored cliffs and rock formations were inspiration to the politicians in Carson City, and in 1935, Valley of Fire was designated a Nevada State Park. It has some of the most spectacular and fascinating geology in the south-western United States and certainly in the great state of Nevada. Bright vermillion-red, layered rock formations are broken, folded and tilted by a vast network of sheer and strike-slip faults.

Violent geological forces displaced entire mountains ranges and moved them more than ten miles from their original locations. The bright red rocks that give the Valley its name are Jurassic Aztec Sandstone, about 180 million years old, the same red rock found in Calico Basin and Red Rock National Conservation Area. In contrast to the youthful Jurassic Aztec Sandstone, is much older Paleozoic limestone and dolomite, in a variety of grey shades. The red rock are the remnants of petrified sand dunes found throughout the south-west, once indicative of a great desert not unlike the Sahara.

Other colorful geologic formations found throughout the valley include Aztec Sandstone and Triassic Chinle Formation near the Arrowhead Trail historic marker, Permian Kaibab Formation about a tenth of a mile outside the west entrance to the park.

Elephant Rock PHOTO: Wynne Benti

WEATHER

Valley of Fire and Lake Mead have the same climate, hot during the summer with daytime temperatures reaching well into the triple digits. Winters are wonderfully mild with temperatures ranging from freezing to 75 degrees. The best time to hike Valley of Fire is winter to spring. Summer thunderstorms, light winter showers and the occasional snowfall contribute an average of four inches of precipitation a year to this dry desert land.

TRAILS

The trails in Valley of Fire are all beautifully planned, very well marked and easy to follow. There are entrance stations on both the west and east sides of Valley of Fire with a daily use fee.

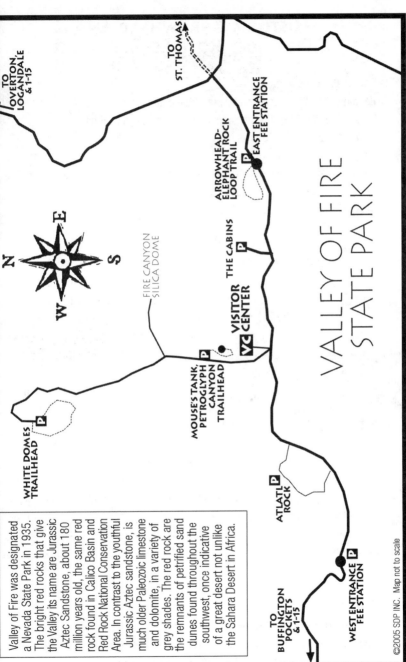

Valley of Fire was designated a Nevada State Park in 1935. The bright red rocks that give the Valley its name are Jurassic Aztec Sandstone, about 180 million years old, the same red rock found in Calico Basin and Red Rock National Conservation Area. In contrast to the youthful Jurassic Aztec sandstone, is much older Paleozoic limestone and dolomite, in a variety of grey shades. The red rock are the remnants of petrified sand dunes found throughout the southwest, once indicative of a great desert not unlike the Sahara Desert in Africa.

TO OVERTON, LOGANDALE & I-15

TO ST. THOMAS

EAST ENTRANCE FEE STATION

ARROWHEAD-ELEPHANT ROCK LOOP TRAIL

FIRE CANYON SILICA DOME

THE CABINS

VISITOR CENTER

VC

MOUSE'S TANK, PETROGLYPH CANYON TRAILHEAD

WHITE DOMES TRAILHEAD

VALLEY OF FIRE STATE PARK

ATLATL ROCK

TO BUFFINGTON POCKETS & I-15

WEST ENTRANCE FEE STATION

©2005 SDP INC. Map not to scale

HISTORIC ARROWHEAD AND ELEPHANT ROCK LOOP TRAIL

Rating: Easy-moderate
Recommended for: Well-conditioned little dogs
Round-trip mileage: 1.5 miles, minimal gain and loss, 1.5 hours
K9 water: No water; 2-quarts minimum
Posted: Pets on leash. Clean up after your pet.
Ambience: Walk along historic road grade promoted as first all-weather route from Salt Lake City to Los Angeles
Best time to hike: October to April.

Driving

Maps: Nevada Road & Recreation Atlas, AAA Las Vegas Vicinity Guide

From the junction of I-15 and US-95 take US-95/US-93/I-515 south to

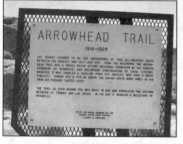

Lake Mead Parkway and exit. Turn left, northeast, and follow Lake Mead Parkway, past Lake Las Vegas to the Lake Mead National Recreation Area entrance station. From the entrance station drive 0.3 miles to Northshore Scenic Drive and turn left towards Callville-Overton. Drive approximately 45.2 miles to the intersection of Valley of Fire State Park Road-169 and turn left, west to the Valley of Fire. Drive 2.0 miles to the fee station and trailhead.

Alternate driving route

From the junction of US-95 and I-15, drive north on I-15 about 32.0 miles to the Valley of Fire State Park-Exit 75. From the exit, head east about 20.2 miles to the Valley of Fire west entrance fee station. Drive about 6.0 miles to the east entrance station and Arrowhead trailhead.

Hiking

The signed trail begins behind the interpretive center. Take the right fork and follow the trail through the bright red rock formations that gave Valley of Fire its name. The narrow trail parallels a power line for a short distance then turns towards the highway where it broadens as it merges with the old Arrowhead Trail road grade, as narrow

Foot bridge across the Arrowhead Trail PHOTO: Wynne Benti

as the cars they were driving back in 1915, the year this section of trail joined St. Thomas and Las Vegas. Cross a metal bridge that spans a narrow red wash. The color of the broken red rock is vivid vermillion. The grade parallels the road and passes the historical marker on the other side of the road that tells the story of the trail. Follow the trail past Elephant Rock to the parking lot.

Notes

The City of Las Vegas laid claim to discovering and building the historic Arrowhead Trail (1914-1924). It was promoted as the first and only all weather route from Salt Lake City to Los Angeles. The one lane road, just wide enough for the narrow cars of the time, received its biggest support from a Los Angeles businessman, Charles H. Bigelow, who drove the road several times in his Packard, which he fondly called "Cactus Kate."

The Cabins, Mouse's Tank & the Petroglyph Canyon Trail

Rating: Super-easy
Recommended for: All dogs
Round-trip mileage: 1.0 mile, 40 minutes
K9 water: No water; 2-quarts minimum
Posted: Pets on leash. Clean up after your pet.
Ambience: Great family hike within the remote recesses of a bandit's hideout
Best time to hike: October to April.

Driving

Maps: Nevada Road & Recreation Atlas, AAA Las Vegas Vicinity Guide

From the junction of I-15 and US-95, take US-95/US-93/I-515 south to

Mouse's Tank Trail   PHOTO: Wynne Benti

Lake Mead Parkway and exit. Turn left, northeast, and follow Lake Mead Parkway past Lake Las Vegas to the Lake Mead National Recreation Area east entrance station. From the entrance station drive 0.3 miles to Northshore Scenic Drive and turn left towards Callville-Overton. Drive about 45.2 miles to the intersection of

Valley of Fire State Park Road-169 and turn left, west to Valley of Fire. (The dirt road to the St. Thomas historic trail is on the west side of this junction). Drive 2.0 miles to the fee station and trailhead. Set your odometer to zero.

0.0	East entrance fee station (Arrowhead trailhead)
1.4	Turn right to The Cabins and shaded picnic area
1.8	Turn right to the Visitor Center and road to Mouse's Tank
1.9	Left fork to Mouse's Tank and White Dome
3.0	Turn right into Mouse's Tank trailhead parking
7.5	End of the road and the White Domes Loop Trail parking area.

Petroglyphs on the way to Mouse's Tank   PHOTO: Wynne Benti

Alternate driving route

From the junction of Hwy. 95 and I-15, head north on I-15 about 32 miles to the Valley of Fire State Park-Exit 75. From the exit, head east about 20.2 miles to the Valley of Fire west entrance fee station. Set your odometer to zero.

0.0	West entrance fee station
6.0	Turn left to Visitor Center and road to Mouse's Tank
6.1	Left fork to Mouse's Tank and White Dome
7.2	Turn right into Mouse's Tank trailhead parking
11.7	End of the road–White Domes Loop Trail parking

The cabins built by the CCC in 1935   PHOTO: Wynne Benti

THE CABINS

These beautiful rock cabins were built in 1935 by the Civilian Conservation Corps just after Valley of Fire became a state park. For years they served as an overnight shelter for folks traveling the long dirt road through Valley of Fire. There is a shaded picnic area.

MOUSE'S TANK AND THE PETROGLYPH TRAIL
Hiking

From the parking lot walk to the signed, well-marked trail just left of the restrooms. The sandy trail winds its way through a narrow canyon used as a hideout by a Southern Paiute Indian named Mouse, best known for his raids on the homesteads of settlers and other Indians in the 1890s. The canyon walls are covered with well-preserved petroglyphs. The walk ends at a deep waterpocket, the Mouse's Tank, used by Mouse as drinking water.

White Domes Loop Trail

Rating: Easy-moderate
Recommended for: All well-conditioned dogs
Round-trip mileage: 1.5 miles, minimal gain and loss, 1 hour
K9 water: No water; 2-quarts minimum
Posted: Pets on leash. Clean up after your pet.
Ambience: The old movie set and slot canyon make this a great trail for the entire family to enjoy. You might even see a gila monster.
Best time to hike: October through April.

Driving
Maps: Nevada Road & Recreation Atlas, AAA Las Vegas Vicinity Guide
See driving instructions for The Cabins, Mouse's Tank & The Petroglyph Trail on previous pages.

Hiking
The trail starts just behind the interpretive sign at the end of the parking lot. Hike the sandy trail between great white sandstone domes on

either side to a series of steps that drop down a narrow gully to the 1965 set of the western, *The Professionals*. This was the hacienda used in the film. Valley of Fire was first used as a backdrop for theatricals in the 1920s. Hal Roach, best known for *The Little Rascals*, filmed many early

...vie set from *The Professionals* PHOTO: Wynne Benti

westerns here. Other films shot on location include: *The Electric Horseman* and *Star Trek Generations*.

The trail drops down into a small wash and turns right, into a high-walled slot canyon. The trails passes through the slot and leaves the wash crossing up and over red sandstone with a fabulous view of miles and miles of bright red rock formations. It gently ascends red rock and loops back to the parking lot.

Slot canyon on the White Domes Trail   PHOTO: Wynne Benti

Notes

We saw a vast array of fabulous lizards on this trail including desert iguana and common collared lizards. The interpretive sign notes the presence of gila monsters, rattlers and scorpions.

Buffington Pockets
Old Man Buffington's Reservoir

Rating: Easy-moderate with some rock scrambling over reservoir
Recommended for: Well-conditioned small dogs
Round-trip mileage: 2.0 miles, minimal gain, 1 hour
K9 water: No water; 2-quarts minimum
Ambience: Beautiful place to set up a ranch and homestead
Best time to hike: October through April.

Driving

Maps: Nevada Road & Recreation Atlas, AAA Las Vegas Vicinity Guide

From the junction of I-15 and US-95, head north on I-15 about 32 miles to the Valley of Fire State Park-Exit 75. Drive east 3.1 miles to a fork and stay right on the Bitter Springs Road, a small stretch of pavement and then good dirt. From this junction head east on the Bitter Springs Road. At 4.3 miles pass some old mining equipment on the left. At 5.2 miles, reach the mouth of the canyon. We like to park here and walk the rest of the way.

Hiking

From the mouth of the canyon, follow the dirt road along the wash up into Buffington Pockets. About 0.8 mile on your right look for a concrete reservoir set off the road against the sandstone. Turn right to the reservoir and pick the easiest way up its right side. Climb over the to the other side and wander through some cat claw and tamarisk to a wide open gravel wash. Continue up the wash past a rock shelter on the left. Soon the story of a great Native American battle, as told to author Florine Lawlor by LaVan Martineau, comes into view.

Notes

Long before cattleman Warren Buffington discovered it in the 1920s, Buffington Pockets, with its remote location, protective overhangs and water source, apparently was the location of a prehistoric conflict between native people, according to author LaVan Martineau. Buffington declared it to be the prettiest place he'd ever seen and immediately built his ranch here. He built the reservoir and parts of the old water pipe down to his house can still be seen.

Rosy at Buffington Pockets PHOTO: Wynne Benti

Las Vegas Dog Parks

OFF-LEASH

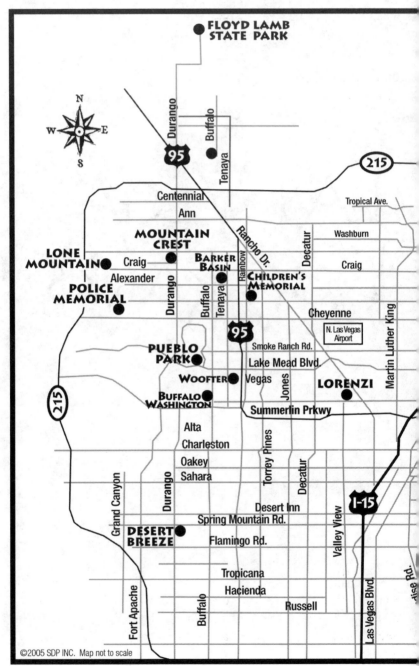

FLOYD LAMB STATE PARK

N
W · E
S

95

215

Durango
Buffalo
Tenaya
Centennial
Ann
Tropical Ave.
Washburn
Decatur
Rancho Dr.
MOUNTAIN CREST
Craig
BARKER BASIN
Craig
LONE MOUNTAIN
Alexander
Durango
Buffalo
Tenaya
Rainbow
CHILDREN'S MEMORIAL
POLICE MEMORIAL
Cheyenne
Martin Luther King
95
N. Las Vegas Airport
PUEBLO PARK
Smoke Ranch Rd.
WOOFTER
Lake Mead Blvd.
Vegas
Jones
LORENZI
BUFFALO WASHINGTON
Summerlin Prkwy
215
Alta
Charleston
Torrey Pines
Oakey
Sahara
Decatur
Desert Inn
Grand Canyon
Durango
Spring Mountain Rd.
Valley View
I-15
DESERT BREEZE
Flamingo Rd.
Tropicana
Hacienda
Russell
Las Vegas Blvd.
dise Rd.
Fort Apache
Buffalo

BARKER BASIN
NORTHWEST

Off-Leash Dog Runs
Address: 7351 W. Alexander Road
Cross streets: Tenaya and W. Alexander

Driving
Map: AAA Las Vegas Vicinity Guide
From the junction of I-15 and US-95, take US-95 north 9.5 miles to Craig Road-Exit 85 and exit. Turn left, west, on Craig Road. Drive 0.3 miles to Tenaya Way and turn left. Drive 0.5 miles to Alexander Road, and park either on Alexander Road or off Tenaya Way.

Description
This wonderful park has eight acres set aside for your dog's delight, with dog fountains and huge fields of lush grass. Three separate areas cater to small, medium and large dogs including the timid and elderly. The dog runs are located in the water detention basin which is normally dry and safe unless there has been a recent intense thunderstorm with an exceptional amount of rain. For those wanting to walk their dogs on-leash, there is a rubberized track that runs a half-mile around the park beneath many nice shady trees. During winter a walk around the water detention basin (there is no shade or water on this part) is approximately one and a half miles around. Bring water. Wayne Bunker Park, in which the dog runs are located, is a full facility park complete with tennis courts, three children's playgrounds, volleyball court, a half-mile rubberized track, picnic areas, restrooms, and a cement skateboard playground.

Looking down into Barker Basin
PHOTO: Megan Lawlor

BUFFALO WASHINGTON
NORTHWEST
(UNNAMED AT PRESS TIME)

Off-Leash Dog Runs
Address: 7901 West Washington Avenue
Cross streets: Buffalo and Washington

Driving
Map: AAA Las Vegas Vicinity Guide
From the junction of I-15 and US-95, take US-95 north to Summerlin Prkwy-Exit 81A. Take Summerlin Prkwy west to Buffalo Drive, exit and turn right, north, then a quick left, west, on Washington Avenue. Drive approximately 0.3 miles just past the fire station and turn left into the parking lot, the closest lot to the dog runs which are on your right as you enter the lot. Turn right and drive west down the parking lot about 0.1 mile to the dog runs on your right (closest to Washington Avenue), the north side of park.

Description
The Buffalo Washington Park is the city's newest and largest park located in the Summerlin area. It's grand opening was September 17th, 2005, and at a cost of $41 million, it spans 110 acres between Buffalo and Durango Avenues.

The off-leash dog runs, located on the north side of the park are some of the biggest in town. These consist of three separate fenced areas, one each for large, medium, and small dogs including puppies, elderly

Gorgeous views and big runs at Buffalo-Washington
PHOTO: Wynne Benti

and physically challenged dogs. They have nice grassy lawns and are full facility with waste bags, doggie drinking fountains and shaded benches for their owners.

Good odors abound PHOTO: Wynne Benti

If you are interested in tennis, this park boasts the largest outdoor tennis center in the state of Nevada. There are twenty-three lighted tennis courts and a tennis center stadium with capacity for three thousand spectators! There is a comprehensive array of tennis programs from beginner to advanced and geared for all ages including, camps, sessions and tournaments. For information on tennis activities phone the Amanda and Stacey Darling Memorial Tennis Center at 702-229-2100. Reservations are accepted for the tennis courts with a nominal usage fee. There are eleven lighted soccer fields, seven with artificial turf. There are two children's playgrounds and several restroom facilities.

Another feature to this park is a two mile paved pedestrian/bicycle path which runs around park. It is about a forty minute walk around. There are waste bags in key locations. Your dog needs to be leashed and there is no water or shade on the path.

CENTENNIAL HILLS PARK
NORTHWEST

Off-Leash Dog Runs
Address: 7101 N. Buffalo Drive
Cross streets: N. Buffalo and Elkhorn

Driving
Map: AAA Las Vegas Vicinity Guide
From the junction of I-15 and US-95, take US-95 north to the Centennial Prkwy-Exit 91. Exit left, east, on Centennial Prkwy to Sky Pointe Drive and turn left. Turn right, north, on Buffalo Drive and go approximately 0.7 miles. The park is on your left, west, just past the fire station.

Description
Centennial Hills Park is a really fun place to take your dog and children. It's just hard deciding which area to go to first! The dog runs are located opposite the children's play area on the north side of the park. There are two big separate grassy runs equipped with dog fountains and shaded benches.

Children's playground at Centennial
PHOTO: Megan Lawlor

The children's playground on the south side of park was designed with great imagination. Here they can play under giant sized colorful flowers and butterflies or climb on gargantuan caterpillars. In the summer when they want to beat the heat they can have fun getting wet in the water play area around huge frog fountains complete with croaking sounds. Swings and three big slides grace the playground. There are ten sand volleyball courts, two soccer fields, a jogging/walking path and restrooms.

Children's Memorial Park
Northwest

Off-Leash Dog Runs
Address: 6601 West Gowan
Cross streets: Rainbow Blvd. and Gowan Road

Driving
Map: AAA Las Vegas Vicinity Guide
From the junction of I-15 and US-95, take US-95 north to Cheyenne. Turn right, east on Cheyenne to Rainbow Blvd, and turn left, north. From Rainbow make a right, east, on Gowan Road. The

Rubberized walking track at Children's
PHOTO: Megan Lawlor

dog runs are located off the middle main entrance to the park. The park extends down to Torrey Pines Road and can be entered from that street.

Description
Plenty of shade and lush grass make this large thirty-acre park a wonderful place to walk. A variety of trees are planted around the park—pine, elm, ash, desert willow and honey mesquite. In summer, orange bird-of-paradise and purple chaste bushes bloom along the soft rubberized track that encircles the park from one end to the other. The walk around the path takes about a half-hour. Dog waste bags are provided for your convenience.

The park has two fenced dog runs, one for large dogs over twenty-five pounds and for small dogs under twenty-five pounds. There are plenty of shade trees with benches and fountains. Other amenities include shaded gazebo picnic tables, barbeques, tennis courts, several baseball fields, four children's playgrounds and restrooms.

Play time at Police Memorial PHOTO: Megan Lawlor

POLICE MEMORIAL PARK
NORTHWEST

Off-Leash Dog Runs
Address: 3250 Metro Academy Way
Cross streets: Cheyenne and Metro Academy (top of West Cheyenne)

Driving
Map: AAA Las Vegas Vicinity Guide
From the junction of I-15 and US-95, take US-95 north to Cheyenne
and exit. Turn left, west, on W. Cheyenne. Drive about 3.5 miles to
Metro Academy Way. Turn right just past the Police Station.
Description
A relatively new park, this twenty-four acre park is located close
to the Las Vegas Metropolitan Police Department's Cheyenne
substation and Challenger private school. The views of Lone
Mountain and the city are fabulous from this area. There are three
fenced, off-leash areas for small, medium and large dogs. The
areas are not terribly huge but the overall ambience is quite pleasant with lots of green grass. There are waste bags and dog drinking fountains. This park is usually not very crowded since it sits
at the top of the city.

Wide open spaces at Woofter   PHOTO: Megan Lawlor

WOOFTER PARK
NORTHWEST

Off-Leash Dog Runs
Address: 1600 Rock Springs Drive
Cross streets: Vegas Drive and Rock Springs

Driving
Map: AAA Las Vegas Vicinity Guide
From the junction of I-15 and US-95, take US-95 north to Rainbow Blvd.-Exit 81B. Take the Rainbow Blvd. exit and turn left. Follow Rainbow Blvd. 0.6 miles to Vegas Drive and turn left, west. Drive approximately 0.2 miles and turn right on Rock Springs Drive. The park is on your left, west.

Description
This little neighborhood park, with nearly nine acres, has a surprisingly large area set aside for leash-free walking. There are three fenced areas for small, medium and large, all with large grassy areas and some trees for shade. Other amenities include dog fountains, waste bags, trash receptacles, a playground for the children and restrooms.

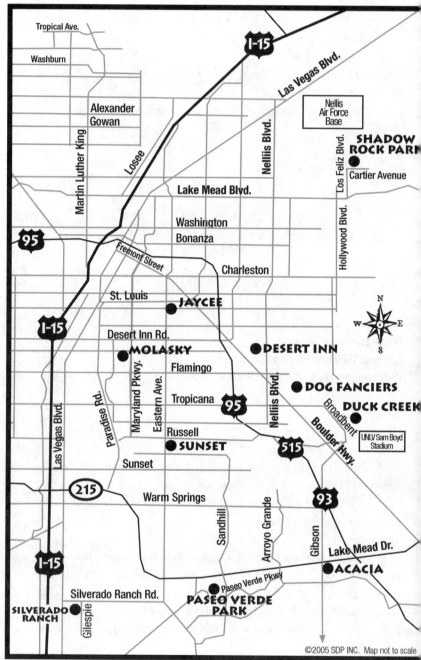

Molasky Family Park
Central

Off-Leash Dog Runs
Address: 1065 East Twain Avenue
Cross streets: Cambridge and Twain, parking off Cambridge and Katie

Driving

Map: AAA Las Vegas Vicinity Guide

From the junction of I-15 and US-95, take I-15 south to Los Angeles and exit on Sahara Ave.-Exit 40, Convention Center. Take the Sahara

Ave., east, to the Convention Center. Follow Sahara about 1.0 mile to Paradise Road and turn right. Drive 0.9 miles to Desert Inn Road and turn left, east. Follow Desert Inn 0.7 miles to Cambridge Street and turn right. Drive 0.5 miles to Twain Avenue. Just past Twain, turn left on Katie Avenue. Parking is 0.1 miles on the left. The dog runs are on the right side of the parking lot, the southeast corner, next to Von's.

Description

Ten-acre Molasky Park is the closest park with off-leash dog runs to the Strip. In fact, from the dog runs you can see the Stratosphere and Wynn's. It has all the amenities—water fountains, waste bags, receptacles, shaded sitting areas and three runs for large, medium, and

The Stratosphere is just one of the casinos that can be seen from Molasky Park
PHOTO: Wynne Benti

small, elderly or the physically challenged canine. There is a Starbuck's in the Von's mall next door.

ALL-AMERICAN PARK
SOUTHWEST

Off-Leash Dog Runs
Address: 1551 S. Buffalo Drive
Cross streets: S. Buffalo Drive and Del Rey

Driving
Map: AAA Las Vegas Vicinity Guide

From the junction of I-15 and US-95, take US-95 north to Charleston Blvd. Drive west on Charleston to Buffalo Drive and turn left, south, to Del Rey and turn right, west, on Del Rey into parking lot across from Social Security Administration office on S. Buffalo.

Description

The park is pleasant enough and suits the off-leash need. There's plenty of grass, water fountains, waste bags, and trash receptacles. The view of buildings, parking lot, and busy Buffalo Drive is somewhat bleak, but the views never seem to bother the dogs!

All-American   PHOTO: Wynne Benti

Shady gazebos, water, grass and good odors at Desert Breeze PHOTO: Wynne Benti

DESERT BREEZE PARK
SOUTHWEST

Off-Leash Dog Runs
Address: 8425 West Spring Mountain Road
Cross streets: At Durango
Driving

Map: AAA Las Vegas Vicinity Guide

From the intersection of the 215-Western Beltway and 159/West Charleston Blvd., head south on the 215 to West Flamingo Road and exit, heading east to S. Durango and turn left. Follow to West Spring Mountain Road. The park is on the right.

Description

This is a huge park spanning both sides of Spring Mountain Road. The dog runs, which consist of an area for small dogs under thirty pounds and a sperate area for large dogs over thirty pounds, are located on the south end of the park and are accessible from either Durango (at Twain Avenue) or Spring Mountain, just past the Desert Breeze Community Center. There are shaded benches, trees, waste baggies, trash cans, and water.

JAYCEE PARK
SOUTHEAST

Off-Leash Dog Runs
Address: 2100 East St. Louis
Cross streets: At Eastern Avenue

Driving
Map: AAA Las Vegas Vicinity Guide

From the junction of I-15 and US-95, head south on US-95/US-93/I-515 to Eastern Avenue and exit. Take to Eastern, right, south to St. Louis Avenue and turn left. The dogs runs are on the right about a block down at Euclid. Park on St. Louis.

Description
This wonderful nineteen acre park within the inner-city of Las Vegas is graced with beautiful old growth trees in its dog runs. Recreational opportunities include baseball/softball fields, playgrounds, basket-

ball court, fitness course, horseshoe, bocce ball and shuffle board courts, jogging and walking paths, picnic areas, restrooms and plenty of shaded open space.

Rosy found a good odor and is about to roll in it   PHOTO: Wynne Benti

DESERT INN PARK
SOUTHEAST

Off-Leash Dog Runs
Address: 3570 Vista Del Monte Drive
Cross streets: Twain and Vista Del Monte

Driving

Map: AAA Las Vegas Vicinity Guide

From the junction of I-15 and US-95, drive south on US-95/US-93/I-515 S to Boulder Hwy.-Exit 70 and exit, left, toward Henderson/Phoenix/Needles. Follow Boulder Hwy./NV-582 S, south, about 1.4 miles to E. Indios Avenue (just past Arizona Charlie's), turn left, then 0.1 miles to Twain Avenue, turn right. Follow Twain 0.2 miles to Vista Del Monte Drive and turn left. The park entrance is about 0.1 mile down on the right. The dog runs are behind the community pool.

Description

A very neat and tidy eighteen acre neighborhood park with a community pool, playground and covered picnic areas. There are waste bags, and water fountains for the dogs, however there was no water fountains in the fountains when we were there—happy we had extra water in the car..

DOG FANCIERS PARK
SOUTHEAST

Off-Leash Dog Runs
Address: 5800 E. Flamingo Road
Cross streets: E. Flamingo and Jimmy Durante Blvd.

Driving

Map: AAA Las Vegas Vicinity Guide

From the junction of I-15 and US-95, drive south on US-95/US-93/I-515 S to Boulder Hwy.-Exit 70 and exit, left, toward Henderson/Phoenix/Needles. Follow Boulder Hwy./NV-582 S, south, and drive 2.0 miles to Flamingo Road (just before Sam's Town Casino) and turn left, east. Follow Flamingo Road for 1.0 miles. You will see a sign for

"Horseman's Park" on your right. Travel 0.2 miles further down Flamingo past this sign and to a stop sign. Turn right at the stop sign and drive 0.3 miles (past the maintenance buildings). The entrance to Dog Fanciers is on the right, west side of street. Park in the dirt lot.

Description

Fun at Dog Fanciers   PHOTO: Megan Lawlor

Almost the entire twelve acres of this park are dedicated to large dog runs. The setting for dog shows and training classes, this is the home of the annual *Strut your Mutt* dog show with plenty of great contests. Besides dog shows, the park is reserved for activities such as canine trials, agility training and club meetings.

The four fenced separate dog runs are all very large with plenty of shade, benches and water bowls strategically placed within the runs. You may want to bring your own as well. Call 702-455-8200 or 455-8264 to reserve the park for a canine-related event.

Sunset Park
Southeast

Off-Leash Dog Runs
Address: 2601 E. Sunset Road
Cross streets: Closet parking is off Eastern Ave.
between Sunset and Warm Springs Road

Driving

Map: AAA Las Vegas Vicinity Guide

From the junction of I-15 and US-95, take I-15 south to the 215-East-Exit 34 toward McCarran Airport/Henderson. Drive 1.9 miles to Exit 8-Sunset Road-McCarran Airport and exit. Drive 0.7 miles and merge

into Paradise Road. Continue 0.6 miles to Sunset Road and exit. Drive 0.2 miles, then turn left on E. Sunset Road/NV-562 E. Follow E. Sunset Road about 1.6 miles east to S. Eastern Avenue and turn right, south (Sunset park is on your left). Just past E. Maule Avenue turn left onto a gravel road-Area F

Sunset Park   PHOTO: Wynne Benti

(unsigned Sunset Park Road). The dog runs are on your left about 0.2 miles down the large gravel parking area.

Description

One of the oldest parks in town, Sunset encompasses nearly 350 acres. The off-leash dog section is located on the far south side of the park, and although the area is small there are sections for different size dogs and the usual amenities—waste bags, receptacles and water fountains. There are enormous open grassy areas around the park for on-leash walking. Large ponds beneath the pines add to the overall ambience. This is a full facility park with lots of activity any day of the week in this park.

Hounds-a-plenty ready to greet the newest visitor PHOTO: Wynne Benti

SILVERADO RANCH PARK
SOUTHEAST

Off-Leash Dog Runs
Address: 9855 S. Gillespie
Cross streets: E. Silverado Ranch Road at Gillespie

Driving
Map: AAA Las Vegas Vicinity Guide
From the junction of I-15 and US-95 take I-15 to SR-160/Blue Diamond Road exit. Take SR-160 east, over the freeway, 0.4 mile to Las Vegas Blvd. and turn right, south. Take Las Vegas Blvd. south 2.4 miles to E Silverado Ranch Road and turn left, east, 0.5 mile to Gillespie and turn right, south, 0.1 mile to the park entrance. The dog runs are on the south end.

Description
For a place that has no grass this was one of the friendliest neighborhood parks in the city. There are two runs, one for timid or small dogs under thirty pounds, and one for large dogs. Amenities include fresh water, waste bags, receptacles and sitting areas.

SHADOW ROCK PARK
NORTHEAST

Off-Leash Dog Runs
Address: 2650 Los Feliz
Cross streets: Los Feliz Street at Cartier Avenue, just off Lake Mead Blvd.

Driving
Map: AAA Las Vegas Vicinity Guide
From the junction of I-15 and US-95 head north to Exit 45a-Lake Mead Blvd., and exit east on Lake Mead Blvd. 6.6 miles to Los Feliz

Big grassy runs and excellent vistas
PHOTO: Wynne Benti

and turn left. Drive 0.6 miles to Cartier Avenue, turn right. The dog run is past the dirt gravel area, at the end of the paved parking area.
Alternate route:
From Boulder Hwy. take Nellis north 5.7 miles to Lake Mead, turn right and drive 2.5 miles to Los Feliz Street, turn left. Drive 0.6 miles to Cartier Avenue, turn right to parking area as described above.

Description
The views are great from this scenic spot next to Sunrise Mountain. High above Nellis AFB and Las Vegas this is a wonderfully pleasant place to exercise your dogs and watch the big planes land at Nellis. There is water, sheltered benches, waste bags, and trash receptacles.

Apparently the only restroom facilities in the park, were the plastic port-a-potties. We were afraid to open them, but we suppose they'll work in a desperate pinch! There's a shooting range up in the hills above the neighborhood and the sound carries on the desert breeze. Shadow Rock tends to be windy and until the perimeter trees mature, gets full sun exposure, so bring your sunscreen!

ACACIA PARK
HENDERSON

Off-Leash Dog Runs
Address: 50 Casa Del Fuego
Cross streets: S. Gibson and Las Palmas Entrada Avenue

Driving

Map: AAA Las Vegas Vicinity Guide

From the junction of I-15 and US-95 take US-95/US-93/I-515 south about 10 miles to Lake Mead Drive-Exit 61 toward Henderson/Downtown. Merge onto NV-146W/W Lake Mead Prkwy. toward Green Valley. Turn left onto S. Gibson Rd. Turn left on Las Palmas Entrada Ave. Turn left yet again on Casa Del Fuego, or pass Casa Del Fuego and turn left directly into the park just off Las Palmas Entrada.

Description

This pretty neighborhood park has a nice setting with a good view of the Black Mountains to the south. The entrance to the park is just off

Scenic views at Acacia PHOTO: Megan Lawlor

Las Palmas Entrada Ave. past Casa Del Fuego. There are benches, three fenced dog runs, one with grass as yet.

There is a playground, water play area (May thru September), lighted ball fields, covered picnic tables, walking course, and a very lovely desert interpretive walk.

DOS ESCUELAS PARK
HENDERSON

Off-Leash Dog Runs
Address: 1 Golden View Street
Cross streets: Desert Shadow Trail at Golden View Street

Driving
Map: AAA Las Vegas Vicinity Guide
From the junction of I-15 and US-95 take I-15 south to the 215-East via EXIT 34 toward McCarran Airport/Henderson. Travel 7.7 miles to the Exit 3-Green Valley Prkwy South. Exit and turn right, south, on S. Green Valley Prkwy to Paseo Verde Prkwy and turn left. Follow Paseo Verde Prkwy to Desert Shadow Trail and turn left to Golden View Street, and turn left. Follow to the park.

Description
This somewhat hidden park gets its name from the two schools located behind it. At press time there was only one very small, fenced dog run with a bench, two shade trees, and as of yet, no grass or canine water fountain. The run, located next to the tennis courts, will certainly satisfy the canine's off-leash need.

PHOTO: Megan Lawlor

Other amenities include a children's playground, ball fields and restrooms.

LAS VEGAS PARKS

ON-LEASH WALKING PARKS

Meandering on-leash paths at Mountain Crest PHOTO: Wynne Benti

MOUNTAIN CREST PARK
NORTHWEST

On-Leash
Address: 4701 N Durango
Cross streets: N Durango and Red Coach, just north of Craig

Driving
Map: AAA Las Vegas Vicinity Guide
From the junction of I-15 and US-95 take US-95 north to Cheyenne Blvd. Go west on Cheyenne to Durango Drive and turn right, north, 1.7 miles to Red Coach Avenue (just past Craig) and turn left. Drive 0.1 mile to the parking lot entrance on right next to community center.

Description
This lovely thirty-eight acre park offers water fountains, canine waste bags and trash receptacles along its meandering concrete paths make it a favorite with local dog walkers. Other features include a unique water fountain playground for children, a shaded pavilion with picnic tables, frisbee golf course, basketball courts and an area at the top of the park for exercising.

FLOYD LAMB STATE PARK - TULE SPRINGS
NORTHWEST

On-Leash
Address: 9200 Tule Springs Road
Cross streets: Off N Durango Drive

Driving
Map: AAA Las Vegas Vicinity Guide

From the junction of I-15 and US-95 take US-95 north to Durango Drive-Exit 93. Turn right on N. Durango Drive and drive 1.3 miles. to Brent Lane, turn right. Drive about 0.4 miles, stay right on Tule Springs Road. Drive 0.2 miles to the entrance gate. There is the standard state park entrance fee. An annual pass may also be purchased. Park hours are 6 a.m. till 7 p.m. in the summer and 6 a.m. till 5 p.m. in the winter. Anyone with a fishing license is allowed to fish with a limit of three fish per person.

Description

Nestled among groves of magnificent cottonwood trees and encompassing 2,040 acres, Floyd Lamb State Park, originally known as Tule Springs, is a remarkable retreat on the outskirts of Las Vegas. Within the park lie four picturesque fishing ponds stocked with catfish and trout. If you are looking for shade and a great place to walk your dog and picnic, this is it. A natural oasis in the stark Mojave Desert, Tule Springs has long been utilized by modern and prehistoric peoples. The history of Tule Springs is quite remarkable. Many people don't realize that this place is one of the earliest prehistoric man sites in the western United States.

Excavated since the turn of the century, Tule Springs was of great interest to archaeologists. In the 1930s two scholars dug up the bones of two ground sloths, a camelops and the partial skeleton of a mammoth. Found among the bones was an obsidian point, a weapon used by prehistoric people. It certainly looked like ancient hunters had killed this ice age animal. These findings were turned over to famed archeologist Mark Harrington, who discovered Gypsum Cave and The Lost City near Moapa, and he was floored. He placed human

Justin and Cinnamon at Tule Springs   PHOTO: Megan Lawlor

occupation of this site at 25,000 years ago. Controversy soon eclipsed his determination, partly because the lack of human artifacts at the site did not substantiate the claims of such lengthy occupation. Still human habitation of Tule Springs dates back 11,000 years. Fossil remains of mammoths, bison, horses, camels, giant sloths and fauna make it one of the best examples of the Pleistocene paleontology sites in Western North America.

The later history of Tule Springs is also interesting and of significance to Las Vegas. Allegedly, in the 1920s the property was rented to bootleggers. In the 1940s, the land was purchased by Prosper Jacob Goumond who turned it into a dude ranch and retreat for guests waiting out their six week residency for a divorce in Nevada. At the time it was the shortest residency requirement for a divorce in any state. After Goumond died in 1954, the ranch was leased as a working cattle ranch until it was purchased by the city in 1964 and renamed for State Senator Floyd Lamb. The park was then acquired

Sneaking a swim on a hot summer's day   PHOTO: Megan Lawlor

by the State of Nevada in 1977 and has remained in its operation since.

Tule Springs has two recreation sections. Both are worth visiting with your dog and children alike. The first part is the southern section. A self-guided interpretive walk takes you around the restored historic ranch and buildings including the prominent water tower.

Drive further to the northern recreation section of the park. This is the best section of the park for shade during the hot summer months. A relaxing retreat within the city to walk your dog, there are picnic tables and grills . This part of the park includes four small fishing lakes (stocked with catfish in the summer and trout during the winter) and groves of shade trees some of which include Aleppo pine, Russian olive, ash and huge cottonwood.

Children will enjoy seeing the peacocks, ducks and geese that live here. Adjacent in this park is the state run nursery where you'll find great buys on trees and other plants. The only draw back to this park is the shooting range nearby. Most of the time you can tune out the noise but if you have a dog that's really gun shy, the best time to go is Monday and Tuesday when the range is closed.

Lone Mountain Peak and Park
Northwest

On-Leash
Rating: Moderate, steep, loose gravel in parts
Recommended for: Small well-conditioned dogs with dog booties
Round-trip mileage: 1.0 miles, 400' of gain, 1-1.5 hours
K9 water: No water on trail; 2-quart minimum
Posted: Pets on leash. Clean up after your pet.
Ambience: Great view of Las Vegas
Lots of dogs on weekends.
Best time to hike: November to April. Get an early morning start.

Driving
Map: AAA Las Vegas Vicinity Guide

From the junction of I-15 and US-95 take US-95 north to Cheyenne and exit, west. Continue 2.0 miles to Durango Drive. Hang a right onto Durango and continue another mile to Alexander Road. Make a left on Alexander and drive another 2.0 miles until you come to Vegas Vista (around Lone Mountain). Make a right onto Vegas Vista and continue to the end of the pavement which is 0.6 miles. Turn slightly right on to the dirt road and drive north to the parking area, 0.1 mile. You can clearly see the trailhead ahead of you. It is on the northwest side of the mountain.

Lone Mountain Park

For those not wanting to make the jaunt up the mountain, Lone Mountain Park, at the base of the mountain is a great place to walk your dog.

Lone Mountain Hiking

The trail starts up a fairly steep rocky part veering towards the right and then levels out onto a ridge (about 15 minutes). We usually stop here with our dogs, take a seat on a bench and enjoy the view of Las Vegas. For people who don't want to continue to the summit, this spot is almost as good as the top. The trail to the summit is to your right (facing south). Pick your way along the trail as it follows the ridge line. It is steep with drop-offs so be careful that your dog doesn't get too

View from Lone Mountain PHOTO: Megan Lawlor

close to the edge. You will come to another flat area and there are several trails but they all lead to the same top. Continue on the use trail up the rocky ridge to the summit. The trail is slippery and loose in places so watch your footing. There are places where a slip could mean a long distance fall. Enjoy the view and retrace your foot steps. The hike may be too rough for dog paws unprotected by dog booties. If so, the park below is wonderful to enjoy.

Notes

If you've lived in Las Vegas for any length of time then you've experienced its fast-paced growth. Just when you think you've found a quiet unpopulated spot in the desert to let your dog run free a neighborhood pops up overnight! Six years ago, the desert behind Lone Mountain used to be that quiet spot. But just as quickly as we found it, it disappeared, replaced by endless rows of houses.

When we were kids, Lone Mountain was a landmark well outside the city, beneath the foothills of the Spring Mountains. There was nothing around it then so it was a prominent feature on the horizon. We rarely ventured out to it because we'd heard rumors of an old hermit who lived in one of its rock shelters who would yell at anyone who came near the peak. Much has changed since those days.

PUEBLO PARK
Northwest

Rating: Easy-moderate
Recommended for: All dogs
Round-trip mileage: 3.5 miles, 1 hours
K9 water: Water fountains along the trail; 1-quart minimum
Posted: Pets on leash. Clean up after your pet. Do not enter if heavy rains or flash floods are in the weather forecast.
Ambience: Great hike for every member of the family
Best time to hike: November to April. Get an early morning start.
Park hours 6 a.m.-11 p.m.

Driving

Map: AAA Las Vegas Vicinity Guide

From the junction of I-15 and US-95, take US-95 north to Lake Mead Blvd. Exit on Lake Mead, west, past Buffalo Drive to Mariner. Make a left u-turn at the traffic light. You will be heading east on Lake Mead. A sign on the right marks the entrance. The park is not visible from the street. After turning right, it is a short drive to the parking area.

Description

This fabulous park lies within a natural desert arroyo. Most of the landscape has been untouched by development, thus retaining its natural beauty. Several Spanish-style homes sit atop the hills above the arroyo, keeping the park well hidden from the streets. All of these features have served to make Pueblo Park exceptionally quiet and peaceful. Most delightfully, the natural setting has allowed many small desert dwellers to remain. One has the sense of having entered the wilderness when walking here. On any given day, squirrels pop in and out of rocky crevices and race across the path. Numerous cottontail rabbits also live in the area.

The first section of the park consists of a children's playground, shaded picnic area with barbeque grills, restrooms and a large grassy field. The path starts here, extending almost 2.0 miles west to its end at Rampart Blvd.

Walking the path along Pueblo Park   PHOTO: Suzanne Villella

The path forks as you pass the first grassy field. Take the one to the left which leads through a tunnel. You will come to yet another pretty section of the park with a second children's playground and grassy field shaded by large cottonwood trees. At the foot of the playground is a low water faucet (not fountain) to give your dog a cool drink.

Lovely, twisted mesquite trees shade the way as you continue along the path. There are benches all along the way. Observing closely, one can usually spot a variety of birds—hummingbirds, sparrows and ravens are most common. Once we were lucky enough to glimpse a hawk quietly soaring above.

Look at the ground ever now and then and you may be able to see an occasional tarantula. These scary looking but harmless spiders are much nicer than they appear. Most are reluctant to bite people unless in self-defense if provoked. Their venom is usually no more harmful than that of a bee. Unwarranted fear and tall-tale stories have given the tarantula an unjust reputation.

Continuing on you will come to the second tunnel under Rampart Blvd. This is the end of the path. There is access by foot at this end but there is no parking. Return the way you came.

Pueblo Park is an enchanting get-away from the city, and well worth visiting.

Lorenzi Park
Where Crawfish Once Swam
CENTRAL CITY

Address: 3333 Washington Avenue at Baker
Rating: Super easy
Recommended for: All dogs
Round-trip mileage: 1.0 miles, flat, 30 minutes
K9 water: 1-quart minimum
Posted: Pets on leash.
Ambience: Shaded inner city park with lake
Best time to hike: Year-round, early morning in summer.

Driving
Map: AAA Las Vegas Vicinity Guide

From the junction of I-15 and US-95, take US-95 south to Valley View and exit. Turn north to Washington Ave. then turn east. Follow Washington past Twin Lakes to Baker and turn right into the parking lot. The lake walk starts behind the buildings at the entrance.

Walking

Follow the shaded foot path around the lake and rose garden. Lorenzi Lake is on the migratory route for Canadian geese. There are picnic

tables and canopied benches along the path, which is also a popular course for runners. The lake is stocked year-round with catfish, trout and bass. The couple we met fishing from their lawn chairs set up along the path said they had yet to see a bass in the many years they have fished the lake (three fish limit).

Near the ranch-style long houses on the north end of the lake is a concrete channel with year-round flowing water. Forty years ago, this concrete and decorative rock channel was a natural bottom creek bed

Rosy waits outside one of the most interesting places in Las Vegas PHOTOS: Wynne Benti

where co-author Megan Lawlor fished for crawfish as a child.

Notes

The day French immigrant, David Lorenzi, arrived in Las Vegas by train in 1911, he saw this location from the depot and immediately set about clearing 80 acres. He discovered a 500 year-old grapevine and began cultivating grapes, fruit trees and vegetables. He decided to build a resort on the property, and began by excavating the lake. Completed in 1922, the lake, then one of the largest manmade bodies of water in Las Vegas, became a popular local attraction.

After Lorenzi sold the property in 1937, subsequent owners built a motel, Twin Lakes Lodge, the low ranch-style long houses along the north edge of the lake. Twin Lakes Lodge was a not only a dude ranch but a place where residents from other states, wanting to take advantage of Nevada's liberal divorce laws could establish the six weeks residency for required for divorce. The State of Nevada purchased the property in 1965.

The Nevada State Museum and Historical Society and Sammy Davis Jr. Festival Plaza are located here, as well as offices for the Nevada State Federation of Garden Clubs and the American Association of Retired People

PASEO VERDE PARK
SOUTH

Posted: Pets on leash. Clean up after your pet.
Address: 1851 Paseo Verde Parkway
Cross streets: Desert Shadow Trail at Paseo Verde Prkwy
Ambience: Lovely on-leash walking path

Driving
Map: AAA Las Vegas Vicinity Guide
From the junction of I-15 and US-95, take US-95 south toward Phoenix/Needles. Drive approximately 13.0 miles to the Lake Mead Drive-Exit 61 to Henderson/Downtown and exit. Drive 0.3 miles and merge onto NV-146 west to Green Valley. Travel 2.3 miles and take the Valle Verde Drive-Exit 2. Drive 0.3 miles to the Valle Verde Drive South ramp. Turn Left onto S. Valle Verde Drive, and drive 0.2 miles to Paseo Verde Prkwy, and turn right to the park.

Description
This very pretty neighborhood park is near the Green Valley District. Although there are no off-leash dog runs, a lovely shaded walking path meanders beneath rose-covered gazebos and around the park.

Paseo Verde PHOTO: Megan Lawlor

This is ten acre park has a large grassy open area, tennis courts, playground, shuffleboard, and volleyball court. If you're in the mood for some coffee, there is a Starbucks down the shaded pathway just east of the park.

The old west almost in the heart of the city PHOTO: Wynne Benti

WETLANDS PARK
DUCK CREEK TRAIL

SOUTH

Rating: Easy
Recommended for: All dogs
Round-trip mileage: 1.25 miles, flat, 40 minutes or less
K9 water: Seasonal water; 1-quart minimum
Posted: Pets on leash. Clean up after your pet.
Ambience: Pleasant walking and jogging within a rare riparian habitat fed by natural seeps and runoff. Lots of dogs on weekends.
Best time to hike: Year-round. Early morning or just before sunset in summer.
Driving

Map: AAA Las Vegas Vicinity Guide

From the junction of I-15 and US-95, take US-95 south to Russell Blvd. Exit and set odometer to zero. Turn left and drive 1.7 miles to Broadbent Blvd. Turn left at Broadbent (passing UNLV's Sam Boyd Stadium on right) then at 2.3 miles, turn right into parking lot at the signed Duck Creek Trail.

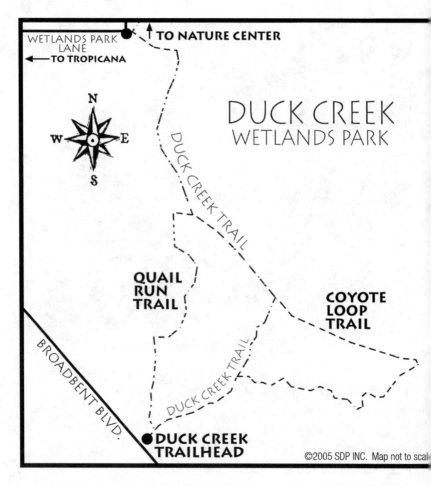

To visit the Wetlands Nature Preserve Visitor Center:

From the entrance to Duck Creek, continue on Broadbent to Wetlands Park Lane, at 2.9 miles, and turn right. At 3.3 miles is the outlet for the Duck Creek Trail (which starts on Broadbent). Dogs are not allowed on any of the trails in the Nature Preserve above the Duck Creek Trail. Continue driving left to the Wetlands Nature Preserve Visitor Center for information and area maps.

Hiking

There are several easy loops that all end the two same outlets for the Duck Creek Trail (at Broadbent) or at Wetlands Park Lane. From the parking lot, walk under the entry way, and follow the wide dirt trail The Duck Creek Trail is straight ahead.

Along Duck Creek Trail PHOTO: Wynne Benti

The Coyote Trail Loop is the first right turn off the Duck Creek Trail coming in from Broadbent. Coyote meanders through tules, tall stands of black-eyed Susans and a small portion of Duck Creek, then merges back into Duck Trail.

The Quail Run Trail cuts through the center of the hiking area, and merges into the Duck Creek Trail. This area is somewhat drier than the nature preserve, but is closed several times a year, mostly in summer, due to flooding. Sun-sheltered benches are strategically positioned throughout the trail area.

Notes

This is the natural, historic, and undiverted channel for water flows through this area, draining into Las Vegas Wash. Dogs were once permitted on the trails in the upper Nature Preserve, however so many unleashed hounds drowned by running off into the tules and getting trapped in deep muddy pools or were killed by coyotes (in front of their owners), Clark County decided to limit canine access to the lower, wider, drier and more visible Duck Creek Trail system.

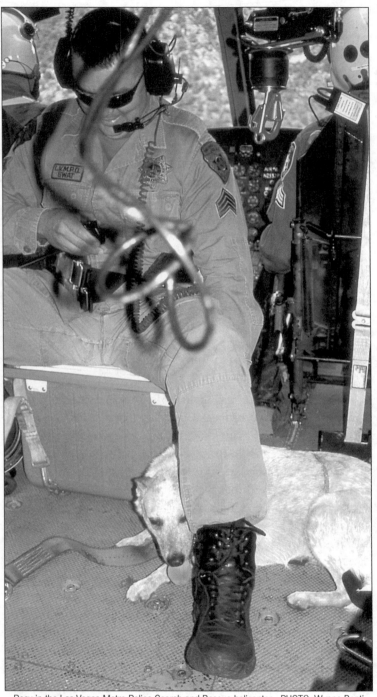

Rosy in the Las Vegas Metro Police Search and Rescue helicopter   PHOTO: Wynne Benti

All In A Day's Work
Scouting Trails for Favorite Dog Hikes in and Around Las Vegas

In a matter of three weeks, Rosy, the cattle dog, and I walked over 300 miles across Southern Nevada. So when we arrived at the edge of the Rocky Gap 4x4 Road in Willow Springs, we had done plenty of four-wheel driving on remote desert roads. The yellow diamond shaped sign at the beginning of the road warned "unmaintained road—travel at your own risk." I've seen those signs before and thought, *we can always turn around.*

The Rocky Gap 4x4 Road, once called the *Old Road to Pahrump* and the *Potato Pass Road*, was in its day, the quickest way from Las Vegas over the mountains to Pahrump. It was a maintained gravel road that started near Willow Springs, summited over Potato Pass, now called Red Rock Summit, then down and out to Lovell Canyon. Author and Las Vegas historian Florine Lawlor recalled as a child driving the road to Pahrump with her grandfather to buy fresh vegetables and fruit. Florine's husband, Jim Lawlor, Sr. drove his Chevy Malibu over the road about fifteen years ago without any problems. During the heavy winter of 2004-05, the road was damaged by washouts, with the worst occurring on the south side, or Pahrump side of Red Rock Summit. Today, the only group that really knows current condition of the road is the Vegas Valley 4-Wheelers and their contact numbers can be found online at <http://www.vv4w.org>.

With a desert peaks guide and two road atlases, we crossed the rugged wash and parked the Jeep at the trailhead for La Madre Spring on the backside of the White Rock Hills. It was August, and when the summer desert sun rises, it bears down with an oppressive heat. Sheltered by the early morning shadows of the White Rock Hills we wandered up the trail. Near the spring we passed a stand of junipers that looked as if they had been neatly planted to line a front yard. Two old soft pink concrete pads indicated that someone else once liked that spot enough to build a pad for a tent cabin. It was in fact, the Depression era Civilian Conservation Corps crew who constructed the catch basin at La Madre Spring. When we reached the spring, a crisp cold water oasis in the heart of the La Madre Mountains, it was still sheltered by morning mountain shadows. Tall stands of non-native bamboo surrounded the little catch basin. We stayed a few minutes then started back down the hill. Along the way we met a woman on her morning walk up to the spring.

We drove on to Red Rock Summit, the trailhead for Bridge Mountain and North Peak. After talking to several people about the condition of the road, the consensus was it was rough in parts, but driveable all the way to Lovell Canyon. Rosy jumped into her usual place, the front passenger seat, and curled up in a ball.

There were rough spots where rainwater from summer storms rushed down a narrow gully from above taking with it part of the road. Embossed in softer sand were the swirling rivulets carved by water on the move. We passed large washes alongside the road, where massive amounts of water had pushed against the tenuous roadside bank, taking rocks, depositing new rocks, tearing away soil from the shallow roots of desert trees. Twisted and broken tree limbs were jammed deep into sand or crushed by boulders.

Rosy got up from her slumber ball to get a better look over the dash. The Jeep, mind you with 250,000 miles on the original transmission and engine, rode right over a long stretch of boulders deeply imbedded in sandy debris. We arrived at Red Rock summit where the familiar design of a Red Rock trailhead sign for

Bridge Mountain and North Peak greeted us.

North Peak was just over a mile away on a pleasant well-worn trail through limestone and junipers covered with silvery blue berries. Fifteen minutes into the trail, I thought, *I never told anyone*

Almost to Red Rock Summit
PHOTO: Wynne Benti

where we were going. I looked at my watch and called a friend's answering machine He was at work so I left a message: *I arrived at Red Rock Summit at 9am and was hiking to North Peak. I planned to go out via Lovell Canyon. We would be back at Bonnie Springs no later than 7pm.* Later, he would tell me my message was incoherent from poor cell reception and he couldn't understand a word.

It was a beautiful day and remarkably cool for August. Thunderheads were already building above us about three hours earlier than usual. We arrived at the cutoff to Bridge Mountain, a drop of about 800 feet over to the sandstone massif. From the saddle, we could see across Bridge Mountain, Red Rock all the way to the Strip. It was hazy, but still a great view. We scrambled up the rugged little summit of North Peak. I looked over at Bridge and read my route description again. We started back down to the car, arriving at 10:30am.

Resetting the odometer to zero, I drove down USFS 549 west toward Lovell Canyon to make the complete loop trip. From Red Rock Summit, the road was in good condition until it joined a wash about three-quarters of a mile down. The last tremendous surge of water and debris through the wash was so violent, it had ripped open a second boulder-filled channel where the road once was. Someone had sprayed-painted black arrows on rocks pointing the way down the new channel. Parking just above the black arrows, I got out of the Jeep to inspect the first obstacle. Rosy sat patiently in the passenger seat. My mistake was, as I realized later, not scouting the entire stretch of wash, not just the first obstacle.

Back in the Jeep, we drove up and over the first obstacle, two large boulders, but not so high that gravity wouldn't pull us down the other side. I drove gingerly down the wash to the next obstacle, large boulders deeply wedged down into the streambed, then a drop-off over a four to five foot high rock wall that someone had

spent a few hours cushioning with small boulders. Too late to turn around—I was committed. Stepping lightly on the gas pedal, the Jeep dropped over the first step of fixed boulders. The front tires pushed a large boulder back, blocking the rear driveshaft. The Jeep stopped, left front tire spinning. The back driver's side panel over the gas cap was inches from a big limestone boulder imbedded in the creek bed. The more I tried to free the car, the closer the back panel got to the boulder.

I turned the off the ignition and Rosy jumped out. For the next hour I tried to raise up the

High-centered on the "Staircase"
PHOTO: Wynne Benti

Jeep up with its tiny stock jack. It just wasn't tall enough to jack the Jeep high enough to get up and over the boulder. I piled rocks under the front and back driver's side tires. When I stepped on the gas pedal, the front driver's side wheel spit out the neatly piled rocks, sinking the Jeep deeper into its shallow grave. I just couldn't get the mechanics right. The back end of the Jeep slid against that big boulder, scraping paint, denting the back panel. Rosy watched from a safe vantage point beneath the shade of a scrub live oak about forty feet down the wash.

It was noon.

Thunderclouds were almost black against the high limestone canyon walls. Rosy and I climbed about 200 feet up the loose steep ridge straight out of the wash above the Jeep with the hope of getting cellular reception. "Call failed" was the only message I got as I repeatedly dialed, then the "battery low" message. It was useless. Any reception was blocked by the steep impenetrable limestone walls all around us. Back at the car I assessed our situation—one apple, a Power Bar (Rosy would get that), eight gallons of water, a sleeping pad, one towel, a thick blanket, a one piece swimsuit, no clothing item warmer, heavier or water repellent than the tee-shirt on my back.

Then it started to rain. The Jeep sat hopelessly impaled in the wash recently devastated by flash floods. I knew when stranded, one was supposed to stay with one's vehicle. With its tenuous position in the wash and visions of motorists stranded by flash floods in the middle of town on the evening news, I wondered whether staying in the wash was the best plan. I plugged the cell phone into the lighter and charged it for twenty minutes, while trying the emergency channel on my CB—nothing. I took off my clothes and put on my swimsuit. If I had to spend the night, I wanted the two pieces of clothing I brought, the tee-shirt and shorts to be dry. I wrote a note on last year's DMV registration card with the date, the time: *Am stranded. Have gone to Red Rock Summit to get cell reception.* I put on my pack and started up the road to Red Rock Summit with Rosy by my side.

All I could think about on the way up was the staff at the Bonnie Springs calling the police when I didn't show up that night. I could see them combing through the contents of my room which included my journal with all of its entries. It was imperative to nip this in the bud.

Thunder echoed throughout the canyons around us. I said to Rosy, thinking of Rip Van Winkle, *it's those fellows playing nine pins.* We hiked back to North Peak, stopping for forty-five minutes in a cold downpour on the trail. Sheltered by juniper limbs, I opened the space blanket I carried in its little package for twenty years and wrapped it around us. Though it was August and hot in the valley, it was unexpectedly cold in the La Madres, with the clouds and the rain at 6,500 feet.

On the summit of North Peak with the Strip in plain view, I held up the phone. Attempts to reach friends failed, so I dialed 911. Once, when we got a flat tire out on an isolated stretch of 395 near Little Lake in California, the only number I could get through to was 911 after all other attempts to call anyone else failed.

The operator patched me through, first to Florine Lawlor, who I thought might have access to a winch or large jack. She didn't and didn't know of anyone who did—that part of her life had ended years ago. Then the operator patched me through to the Auto Club. I told them I needed a winch and that once I left this spot, there would be no cell phone reception, no wat to contact me. I naively thought, with all the desert around and all the SUVs in Las Vegas, that backcountry desert service would be standard procedure for the Auto Club—not quite.

We hiked back down to the Jeep. Rosy climbed in the back and immediately fell asleep. *We will hike out to Willow Springs tomorrow,* I thought. I was too tired. Then I heard that unmistakable sound, that thunderous sound of a helicopter. *Oh, no, not a helicopter–a jack, a winch, yes– but not a helicopter.*

The helicopter with its round front light glowing brightly through the dark afternoon clouds, came down the canyon and hovered above the Jeep. A Las Vegas Metro Police officer dropped down in front of us. I said, *I didn't call for a rescue, just a winch.* He told me, when the Auto Club driver couldn't find me, the Auto Club called Search and Rescue. *We can't leave you here now. You have to come with us.* Not exactly what the author of a hiking guide wants but they were doing what they do best and doing it well.

I grabbed what I could out of the Jeep. The three of us walked down the wash to a more open location where the helicopter could land. He put a harness on Rosy who was freaked out by the noise and the wind kicked up by the helicopter blades. When she started to resist his gentle efforts, he grabbed her by the scruff of the neck and tossed her gently into the helicopter. Rose lost her bowels as she hit the floor of the helicopter. I climbed in and we were off over the spectacular scenery of Red Rock. They dropped us off at the visitor center which was closed. The officer suggested I might want to get the vehicle out soon, as it would be stripped eventually. He handed me a piece of yellow paper with the GPS coordinates and a reminder note—*your car is at . . .*

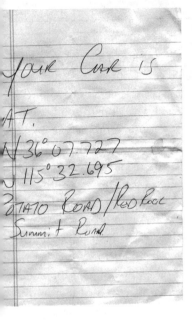

A tourist offered me a ride back to the dog-friendly Bonnie Springs Motel in the heart of Red Rock where we were staying. I opted to wait for Florine Lawlor, Leslie Payne and my coauthor's daughter, little Annie, who were coming to get us.

As we waited for them at the closed entrance station I noticed a piece of paper taped to the window, "Rocky Gap 4x4 Road closed due to storm damage." *How did I miss that sign*, I thought. While I sat there, people who were entering the park after hours kept stopping thinking I was collecting the entry fee. Finally, I just started waving people through. Must have been the faded green hiking shorts and high boots that gave me the official ranger-like appearance.

The next morning, I called local tow truck drivers who advertised four-wheel drive recovery. They wanted upwards of $1500. So I called a friend who went online and found a contact number for the Vegas Valley 4-Wheelers. Within an hour, one of their members, Edwin Moradian, on his day off, picked me up at the Bonnie Springs in his Mercedes Benz UNIMOG. We drove back over the Rocky Gap Road via Willow Springs to the Jeep. Along the way, we passed a mountain biker coming up from Lovell Canyon. We asked if he saw my car and he laughed:

Good luck getting it out, he said.

Eventually, we arrived at the sad, lonely looking Jeep. Within

Edwin Moradian of the Vegas Valley Four-Wheelers
PHOTO: Wynne Benti

minutes, Edwin jacked it up and placed rocks beneath the passenger side wheels, in fact, completely opposite of the mechanics I attempted the day earlier. Then he stood in front of the Jeep, and directed me to depress the brake while stepping on the gas pedal.

With Rosy in the passenger seat, the Jeep zipped right up and over the big boulder and down the infamous geological anomaly known as the "staircase."

Edwin spotted me the entire way down the wash. He stood in front of the Jeep before each obstacle and motioned with either hand, which way to turn the wheels—forward, left, right, stop. Up and over angled walls of loose gravel, barely fitting a tire across precipitous edges, one wheel placed on a narrow rock three feet high and as wide as the tire. Then finally, terra firma—the dirt road on the other side of the wash, smooth and welcoming.

And then, that was it—we were out. In minutes we were at the junction of USFS 549 and the paved Lovell Canyon Road. From there it was a painless drive on pavement all the way back to Las Vegas. I asked Edwin if there was something I could do to repay him. He said, *Just send a check to the club for $10. Write on it, two Coronas for Edwin at the next meeting.*

INFORMATION

IMPORTANT CONTACT NUMBERS

Las Vegas Metropolitan Police Department Search and Rescue (LVMPD SAR)
2990 N. Rancho Dr.
Las Vegas, Nevada 89130
702-229-3567
http://www.lvmpdsar.com/officerprofile.html

The Las Vegas Metropolitan Police Department Search and Rescue unit is one of the best in the country. Since they were the largest and only cohesive police force in this desert area for years they handled all Search and Rescue for the entire Clark County region. If you are stranded, trapped or otherwise in need of rescue, these officers and the volunteers that dedicate their time to this group will be the ones who come to your aid. Unfortunately, the BLM and USFS must spend most of their time enforcing regulations on public lands and do not have staff or funding for any rescues. *A call to 911 will engage the help of LVMPD SAR.*

Emergency 911

Even with Las Vegas in eyesight, cell phone service is non-existent in many of these remote desert areas. We once stood on the summit of North Peak, with a direct shot to the strip and were only able to get through to 911 Emergency— which was a good thing. Generally, if you are in a canyon, you'll need to get to a highpoint to get cell phone reception and in most cases, you need to keep punching in 911 if you are unable to contact anyone else. It is important carry a map, to know where you are, and have alternate plans just in case it is not possible to reach outside help.

Desert National Wildlife Refuge
Desert NWR
HCR 38, Box 700
Las Vegas, NV 89124
Email Address: Amy_Sprunger-Allworth@fws.gov
Refuge Phone: 702-879-6110
Fax: 702-879-6115

Las Vegas
Nevada State Museum & Historical Society
700 Twin Lakes Drive
Las Vegas, Nevada 89107
Phone: 702-486-5205
Fax: 702-486-5172

Lake Mead
Lake Mead National Recreation Area
601 Nevada Highway
Boulder City, Nevada 89005
Phone (702)293-8907
Web Site - www.nps.gov/lame

Alan Bible Visitor Center
US 93 and Nevada 166
Four miles north of Boulder City
702-293-8990

Boulder City Museum and Historical Association
Located in the Boulder Dam Hotel
1305 Arizona Street, Boulder City, Nevada 89005
P.O. Box 60516, Boulder City, Nevada 89006-0516
Phone: 702-294-1988 | Fax: (702) 294-4380
Email: info@bcmha.org

Lost City Museum
721 S. Moapa Blvd.
PO Box 807
Overton, Nevada 89040
702-397-2193

Pahranaghat National Wildlife Refuge
Pahranaghat NWR
PO Box 510
Alamo, NV 89001
775-725-3417
http://desertcomplex.fws.gov

National Wildlife Refuge Information
1-800-344-WILD (9453)
http://www.fws.gov

RED ROCK
Red Rock National Conservation Area
HCR 33, Box 5500
Las Vegas, NV 89124
702-363-1921
http://www.blm.gov/nhp/index.htm
Note: At press time (September 2005), the BLM's site was being redesigned to increase its security. As a result, the Red Rock pages were not available.

BLM Red Rock Canyon NCA Climbing Rangers
702-515-5138 or 702-515-5042

Red Rock Canyon Interpretive Association
BLM Visitor Center
Red Rock Canyon NCA
159 & Red Rock Canyon NCA Scenic Loop
http://www.redrockcanyonlv.org/

Friends of Red Rock Canyon
P.O. Box 97
Blue Diamond, NV 89004
702-255-8743
http://www.friendsofredrockcanyon.org

SPRING MOUNTAINS
Humboldt-Toiyabe National Forest
Spring Mountains National Recreation Area
4701 N. Torrey Pines Drive
Las Vegas, NV 89130
702-515-5400
http://www.fs.fed.us/r4/htnf/districts/smnra.shtml

VALLEY OF FIRE
Valley of Fire State Park
P.O. Box 515
Overton, Nevada 89040
702-397-2088

ESSENTIALS FOR DAYPACK & VEHICLE

- Map (7.5 minute USGS topographic maps for specific area)
- Compass
- Sunglasses (and a spare pair)
- Sunscreen
- Hat (brimmed, light-colored to reflect the sun)
- Water (at least 2-4 liters minimum) with electrolyte replacement powder and energy food/snacks/lunch
- Clothing. Dress in layers. Include lightweight rain jacket/pants that can double as a windbreaker; lightweight polypropylene or other synthetic underwear, tops and bottoms; synthetic or wool sweater
- Pocket knife
- Matches in a waterproof container or plastic baggie
- Flashlight
- First-aid kit with the following basic items:
    - Waterproof tape (good for wrapping heels and toes to prevent blisters)
    - Moleskin (good for wrapping heels and toes to prevent blisters)
    - Neosporin (anti-bacterial ointment)
    - Alcohol pads
    - Blistex (or other anti-chapping ointment)
    - Small bottle of bug repellent
    - Tweezers (for removing cactus spines)
    - Needle-nose pliers (for removing cholla spines)
    - Roll of gauze/gauze pads; ace bandage (for sprains)
    - Band-aids
    - Whistle
    - Aspirin (or acetaminophen for high altitude—not as apt to cause stomach upset)
    - Antacid for stomach upset (for high-altitude)
- Sturdy boots with insoles
- Cell phone

Basics for the car (refer to "Desert Roads" on page 33 for additional information):
- Road map (AAA maps or Nevada Road & Recreation Atlas, Benchmark Maps)
- Water (at least six to eight gallons, in separate containers, for two people on one waterless weekend)
- Tire jack, spare tire, lug wrench, tool kit, battery jumper cables, roll of duct tape, tow-rope
- Can of puncture seal (for emergency flats when the spare has been used)
- Cooler (with fruit juices, soda, preferably with sugar, sports drink like Gatorade)
- 2 two to three foot long two by four boards (for tires that get stuck in sand)
- Small shovel

Basics for the overnight car camp:
- Water (extra containers)
- Roll-away camp table
- Camp stove
- Lawn chairs
- Ground cloth
- Sleeping bags (good for wrapping cooler during day to insulate and keep cool in car from sun)
- Sleeping pads
- Firewood & metal tub or garbage can lid (for campfires where permitted)
- Tent

BIBLIOGRAPHY

Benchmark Maps, *Nevada Road & Recreation Atlas*, Benchmark Maps, Canada 2003

Clinesmith, Larry L., and Sellars, Elsie L., *Red Rock Canyon Plants,* Red Rock Canyon Interpretive Association, Las Vegas, NV 2001

Desert Peaks Section, Sierra Club, Dave Jurasevich, editor, *Road and Peak Guide*, Fourth Edition, Los Angeles CA 1997

Dodge, Natt A., *Poisonous Dwellers of the Desert,* Sundance Press, Tucson, 1986

Hanson, Jonathan and Roseann B., *Fifty Common Reptiles & Amphibians of the Southwest*, Western National Parks Association, Tucson, AZ 1997

Khan MD., Asad, Fellow, *Naegleria,* Department of Internal Medicine, Division of Infectious Diseases, Louisiana State University Health Science Center, 2003

Lawlor, Florine, *Out From Las Vegas, Adventures A Day Away,* Spotted Dog Press, Bishop CA, 2002

MacMahon, James A., *Deserts*, Alfred A. Knopf, Inc. NY 1992

Martineau, LeVan, *The Rocks Begin to Speak*, KC Publications, Las Vegas 2003

Nevada Bureau of Mines and Geology, *Geologic Tours in the Las Vegas Area, Special Publication 16,* Mackay School of Mines, University of Nevada Reno, 2001

Nevada Division of State Parks, *Valley of Fire,* Carson City, NV 2005

Rusho, W.L., *Everett Ruess A Vagabond for Beauty,* Gibbs Smith Publisher, Salt Lake City UT 1983

McBride, Terry, *This Was Nevada: Slavery in Nevada,* State of Nevada Department of Cultural Affairs, State Historic Preservation Office

Stewart, Jon Mark, *Mojave Desert Wildflowers*, Albuquerque, NM 1998

Taylor, Richard B., *Mt. Charleston History Vol. 4*, Beehive Press, Las Vegas NV

University of Edinburgh, *Naegleria, Pathogenicity of Naegleria*, 2003

University of Nevada, Reno, Special Collections, *A Guide to the Wheeler Survey Field Notebooks of the U.S. Geographical Survey West of the 100th Meridian Collection No. NC319*

Wheeler, George M., *Preliminary Report Concerning Explorations and Surveys Principally in Nevada and Arizona... Conducted under the Immediate Direction of 1st Lieut. George M. Wheeler, Corps of Engineers. 1871. F 841 .A33.*

Wheeler, George M., *Annual Report upon Geographical and Geological Explorations and Surveys West of the One Hundredth Meridian in California, Nevada, Utah, Arizona, Colorado, New Mexico, Wyoming, and Montana. 1874. 917.8 Un581a.*

Zdon, Andy, *Desert Summits: A Hiking and Climbing Guide to California and Southern Nevada,* Spotted Dog Press, Bishop CA, 2000

INDEX

ABOUT THE AUTHORS

WYNNE BENTI

Wynne Benti, author, *Favorite Dog Hikes In and Around Los Angeles*, and *Climbing Mt. Whitney*, splits her time between Las Vegas and Bishop. She has always hiked with her dogs, adopted from shelters or rescued. Awarded the Desert Peaks Section list finisher pin in 1995, Benti has hiked in Las Vegas and Nevada for two decades. She has

Wynne Benti, Rosy and Megan Lawlor

climbed more than 400 peaks in the Southwest and made ascents of Nevada's highest peak, Boundary, and the highest in Clark County, Charleston Peak, Mummy, Stirling and Hayford, each more than once. In 1990, she founded the Sierra Club's K9 Committee based in its largest chapter in Los Angeles and conducted dog hiking clinics at REI. She is often a guest speaker at animal

shelter fundraisers. Rosy, Benti's two year-old cattle dog has climbed White Mountain Peak (14, 256′), Charleston Peak and Mummy.

MEGAN LAWLOR

Las Vegas native, Megan Lawlor, has been hiking Las Vegas with her dogs since she was a child. Lawlor and her family have a long history in Las Vegas, that includes pioneering railroad men and gold miners. She hiked Red Rock when the scenic loop was a remote dirt road miles from town. She is one of the few Las Vegans who can say that a gila monster walked into their living room!

Daughter-in-law to Las Vegas' beloved author and retired Las Vegas Sun/Review Journal columnist, Florine Lawlor, who wrote the enduring series *Out From Las Vegas: Adventures A Day Away*, Megan loves her town and knows Las Vegas for the great outdoor opportunities that abound here.

Together Benti and Lawlor have over 50 combined years of desert hiking experience!

OTHER GREAT BOOKS

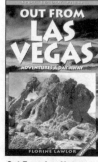
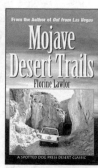

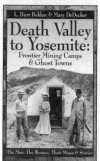